HERMANN BECKH (Sanskrit, becoming Professor of Oriental Studies at the University of Berlin. A master of ancient and modern languages, he wrote extensively on religious and philosophical subjects, including Buddhism, Indology, Christianity, Alchemy and Music. In 1911, he heard a lecture by Rudolf Steiner and was inspired to join the Anthroposophical Society, where he soon became a valued co-worker. In 1922, he helped found The Christian Community, a movement for religious renewal. His many books are gradually being translated from the original German and published in English.

THE ESSENCE OF TONALITY

An Attempt to View Musical Subjects in
the Light of Spiritual Science

and

THE PARSIFAL=
CHRIST=EXPERIENCE

in Wagner's Music Drama

Hermann Beckh

Translated by Alan Stott and Anneruth Strauss

TEMPLE LODGE

Temple Lodge Publishing Ltd.
Hillside House, The Square
Forest Row, RH18 5ES

www.templelodge.com

First published as a single volume in English by Temple Lodge 2022

Previously published as two separate books by Anastasi Ltd. in 2001 and 2015

Originally published in German as three books: *Vom Geistigen Wesen der Tonarten* Verlag Preuss & Jünger, Breslau 1922, *Das Christus-Erlebnis im Dramatisch-Musikalischen von Richard Wagners Parsifal*, Die Christengemeinschaft, Stuttgart 1930, and *Richard Wagner und das Christentum*, Verlag der Christengemeinschaft, Stuttgart 1933

A CIP catalogue record for this book is available from the British Library

ISBN 978 1 912230 89 1

Cover by Morgan Creative
Typeset by Symbiosys Technologies, Visakhapatnam, India
Printed and bound by 4Edge Ltd., Essex

Contents

Part 1

THE ESSENCE OF TONALITY

Preface

This essay is written for those who have not only a general understanding or interest in music, but also a feeling for the keys and their individual, differentiated colourings, and who can experience them inwardly. It is written for musicians and music-lovers who, because of their particular musicality experience something spiritual, and for spiritual seekers and sensitive people who, because of their particular spirituality, have experienced a connection with music. The facts and connections indicated here are in themselves not really new. Through the method of observation attempted here, they might be viewed in a new light. This short work does not claim to have exhausted the subject. It would hope to stimulate the thoughtful reader to further work on these inner considerations and questions.

Hermann Beckh
Breitbrunn, July 1922

Preface to the second edition

The friendly interest that this essay has met with in wider circles has made it possible for a further edition to appear. Apart from a few significant changes and additions—especially some new and revealing musical examples of certain keys—the content of the first edition has been retained.

Hermann Beckh
Stuttgart, October 1925

Preface to the third edition

The new edition of the little book, which had already become a necessity in the spring of 1930, was unpleasantly delayed as a result of many other, larger works by the author. The whole thing was again thoroughly worked through and revised, enriched by many details, improved and corrected in many points. Much that could only be hinted at here is to be presented in more detail in a separate work entitled 'The spiritual meaning of the musical keys in Richard Wagner'.[1]

Hermann Beckh
Stuttgart, 1st March 1932

Translator's Preface

The present monograph on the musical keys (1922, 1932) may appear at first glance to be a reactionary pamphlet, an attempt to justify our musical system under onslaught from the avant-garde of the day who regarded the system of musical keys as redundant. *The Essence of Tonality*, however, is an informed attempt by a universal scholar to establish tonality as a basic key—no pun intended—for cultural renewal, penned at a time when all culture was under threat of becoming lawless.

Prof. Hermann Beckh (1885-1937) chose music, not only because he was literate in the music from Europe of the previous 400 years and could play on the piano all the musical works known to music-lovers of the time. *The Essence of Tonality* was first presented as a lecture (Breitbrunn, August 1922) to the founders of The Christian Community. He joined this 'Movement for Religious Renewal', recognizing his ordination as the goal of his life's search. Fifteen years later, approaching his end on his sickbed, faced with the request to translate more ancient texts for which he was more well-known, he nevertheless decided rather for music, to bequeath something 'for the future'. And so he revisited his early essay on tonality, vastly expanding it into a comprehensive survey of what amounts to the musical repertoire 'from Bach to Bruckner', with particular detailed reference to Wagner's music dramas. The work was posthumously published (1937) as *Die Sprache der Tonart*—in English, *The Language of Tonality* (Anastasi 2015, re-issue TL forthcoming).[2] Most of the first German edition was pulped by the Nazis. Heinrich Himmler, Leader of the SS during the Third Reich, admitted in a letter (30 June 1942) that Beckh was 'an excellent researcher' and praised his book on Buddhism (1916). Himmler, however, went on, and, blaming Rudolf Steiner's anthroposophy, dismissed Beckh in a breath. Similar prominent Nazis, like Jakob Wilhelm Hauer, found the anthroposophical world-view 'directly opposed to National Socialism'.

Beckh was no academic recluse. He left the Humboldt University in Berlin (Nov. 1921), at a time of widespread unrest and uncertainty, convinced that cultural renewal comes only from individual spiritual research. Anthroposophical research, he pointed out in detail in his farewell lecture, is to balance out the obvious and acknowledged material developments of civilization.

The basic thought of *The Essence of Tonality* is the correspondence of the circle of fifths (the keys) to the zodiac. Research is to be directed, not to the abstract twelve chromatic *notes* of atonality, but towards the twelve vital, spiritual *key-centres* as expressing the cosmic rhythms in which we all evidently live—daily, weekly, monthly, annually and even longer rhythms. Beckh appeals to centuries-old tradition—nothing to do with any popular conceptions or misconceptions—without here going into the details that inspired the ancient world and the religious and artistic life of Medieval and Renaissance Europe. Beckh believed a spiritual view of tonality would ensure its—and humanity's—future. Beckh himself claimed many times that his insights into the spiritual archetypes all derived from his musical approach—he called it 'my theme'. Back in 1922, as far as can be ascertained, Rudolf Steiner was present when Beckh repeated his lecture in Stuttgart. Beckh, full of enthusiasm, paid no attention to the clock, yet Steiner, it is reported, remained to the end. Some weeks later Steiner gave a unique lecture (Dornach, 2 Dec. 1922, in GA 283, Am. tr. *The Inner Nature of Music*, Anthroposophic Press 1986), amounting to the esoteric basis of the musical professions.

The Translator's Introduction to *The Language of Tonality* already discusses Beckh's relevance for the twenty-first century. Here we may mention some of his subsequent research (1922–1937).

Hermann Beckh hoped to create access to the Mysteries from which he was convinced renewal had always flowed. When Arthur Drews and other materialistic philosophers claimed to have found in Mark's Gospel an 'astral myth'—concluding that Jesus had never walked on the Earth—Beckh's colleagues pressed him to answer the challenge. At first reluctant, he eventually agreed as the only one equipped or capable of undertaking the task. The result was *Mark's Gospel, the Cosmic Rhythm* (1928. Eng. ed. TL 2021), followed by a sequel *John's Gospel, the Cosmic Rhythm* (1930. Eng. ed. TL 2021). Both works present a vastly superior account of the challenge presented to the twelve disciples, who represent humanity, culminating in a totally original approach to the origin and meaning of the eternal gospel.

When writing his magisterial work, his 'Contributions to a new Star Wisdom', *The Language of the Stars* (1930-32), Beckh relaxes from his impersonal style. This duplicated series he intended to polish for publication. The original text has been translated into English (TL 2020), together with a study on the twelve sentences of the renewed Creed of The Christian Community 'for readers of Beckh's books' penned by Rudolf Frieling. Dr Frieling was to steer The Christian Community from 1960 to 1986.

Beckh also wrote a study on Wagner's *Parsifal* (1930. Eng. ed. 2022, with the 1933 'Wagner and Christianity'), which music drama he first experienced in Bayreuth as a sixteen-year-old. It was decisive for his life. Along with *Tristan and Isolde*, dear to his and the composer's heart—the major work discussed in *The Mystery of Musical Creativity* (TL 2019)—he regarded these music dramas as heralding a Mystery-art of the future. Not only in work collected in *The Source of Speech* (TL 2019) and in *From the Mysteries* (2020) and *Collected Articles* (TL forthcoming, 2023), but specifically in interpreting music, the Gospels and finally establishing a Christian star wisdom, as was Rudolf Steiner's wish (Prof. Beckh was present at Dr Steiner's lecture-course, *Christ and the Spiritual World and the Search for the Holy Grail*, Leipzig, 1913), Beckh's achievement is all of a piece and all is now available in English translation.[3] This unique lifetime's work to reveal vital and essential structures—present in seed-form in *The Essence of Tonality*—has not yet been equalled up to our own day.

One or two points of detail have been noted in endnotes distinguished from the authors own by '*Tr. note*'; some suggested further reading is also offered at the end. My grateful thanks to Neil Franklin and Katrin Binder for many helpful suggestions and much more—and indeed for collaborating throughout on the English translations of Beckh's Collected Works. Any remaining blemishes are due to my inadequacies.

Alan Stott
All Souls' Day, 2021

1

A spiritual investigation into the controlling factors within the system of keys links up with the traditional theory of music at three important points, for the very reason that this theory comes from a time when a certain feeling for spiritual connections was more prevalent than it is today. The first point is the usual division into keys with sharp and those with flat notes. From a purely logical standpoint it might appear that this is merely conventional and arbitrary, and that another system of notation might well be found that is not built upon this duality. But a spiritual point of view, if we can manage to attain it, shows that this difference is based on spiritual reality. This forms the basis of the following essay. 'Proofs' can only arise out of the way in which the whole exposition hangs together, for those who are able to build it together into a living picture.

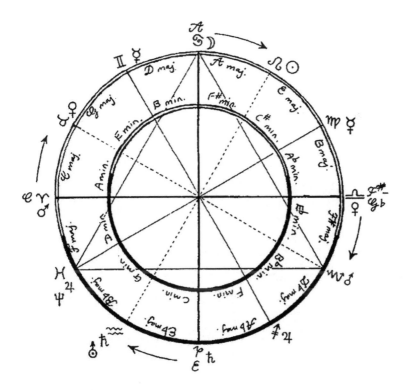

Fig. 1

A second point in which spiritual experience corresponds with the prevalent theory of music is the building-up of the key-system in the ascending circle of fifths. The third point, where the inner connection is easiest to see, is the connection of the major key with its relative minor, that is, to the minor key whose tonic lies a minor third below that of its relative major. The difference between the keys with sharps and those with flats, the circle of fifths, and the relation of the major to the minor keys are the basic elements from which Fig. 1 above is built. This contains in essence everything which will be developed more fully in the following exposition on the spiritual question of the keys.

Apart from these three points, a fourth element important to the spiritual view under consideration here is a certain directed movement, indicated by an arrow in the diagram. The circle of keys is not to be imagined as static but as permeated by inner movement. It is then apparent that certain keys have something 'ascending', others something 'descending' peculiar to them, a tendency not of course to be looked for physically but only spiritually. With this the spiritual view of the system of keys proposed here is one of a circle of twelve keys in inner movement—twelve major keys with their twelve relative minor keys—and in this sense it is possible to speak of 'an archetypal unity of twelve keys'.

Before we can continue with actual spiritual observations, an obvious objection that can be raised against this circle of keys, against this 'archetypal unity of twelve', must be refuted. It could be said—and this objection seems to be justified—that this constellation of twelve keys is not at all the actual musical reality, which in fact contains a much larger number of keys. The circle of twelve is simply taken from the piano, whose tempered tuning does not take into consideration the difference between C# and D♭, D# and E♭, F# and G♭, and so on. The whole circle of twelve keys, then, is only built upon the appearance of the keyboard and not on the reality of the notes themselves. Now, the difference between C# and D♭, between F# and G♭, and so on, is much too well-known to be the subject of argument or discussion and nowhere in this exposition will it be denied. It is indeed true that nothing in itself hinders us from going from F#-major in the circle to C#-major, and it would be arbitrary and conventional to remain at C#-major. But as we can go from F#-major to C#-major, so we can go further from C#-major to G#-major, D#-major, A#-major, E#-major, B#-major, and so on. In such a progression the circle of fifths never comes to a close, and we continue on, so to speak, in a spiral, as is shown in Fig. 2. Theoretically there are no limits to this continuing spiral; from B#-major we could go on to Fx-major, Cx-major, Gx-major, and so on. But instead of this, we could close the circle when we make the transition from B# to the enharmonic C-major. and from there come to G-major, D-major, and so on, and back again to F#-major on the opposite point of the circle. Then opposite the first circle of keys, which leads from C-major to F#-major and from there through keys with flat notes back to C-major, we could place an F#-major/C#-major circle and, of course, a G♭-major/C-major circle and other chromatic-enharmonic circles of keys, but then we must be careful not to step beyond the bounds of reality. But these chromatic–enharmonic circles of keys will always be based on the constellation of twelve, and for that spiritual view there will always be a unity of twelve keys in which the circle of keys is enclosed.

It could not be said that such keys as C#-major, G#-major, D#-major, and so on, or other similar formations in the realm of the flat keys, have no practical meaning. As transition keys they indeed play an important part in modulation, and in actual musical works they frequently

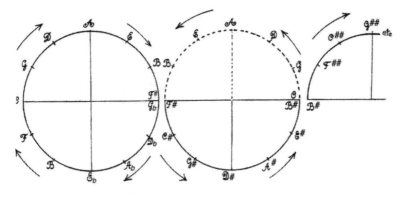

Fig. 2

appear in the development sections. In the choice of a home key for a piece of music, it is actually not common to go beyond C#-major and C♭-major (seven sharps and seven flats respectively). The key of C#-major especially does undeniably possess a certain meaning as a home key. Bach characteristically preferred this to the darker, romantic D♭-major. In both books of *The Well-Tempered Clavier* (WTC), the Preludes and Fugues following those of C-major and C-minor are in C#-major, not D♭-major. Such a key as C#-major will by no means be excluded from the present attempt at spiritual observation. But it must be recognized as a part of another, a second circle of keys that arises as a chromatic-enharmonic circle of twelve, above or next to the first. With this further circle of keys the relations will not be the same but analogous to the first (only the direction of movement inside the circle is different). There is consequently no essential practical need to include it in these observations. Everything essential about a spiritual view of the system of keys can be developed from the basic circle of twelve from which we begin, and which also *essentially* covers the circle of keys conventionally used for musical compositions. Making appropriate use of what is gained here from the chromatic-enharmonic circle of keys may rest with the reader. It cannot be the basis of objection to the chosen point of departure.

It is hardly necessary then to stress that when we put the keys F#-major and G♭-major on that point on the circle opposite the key C-major, we are not saying that they are the same. But the transition, so to speak, must first be found from F# to G♭ at this place if the transition from the keys with sharp notes to those with flat notes in the order on the circle is to come about. The same happens if we arrive from above at F#-major, or from below, from the circle of keys with flat notes via Gb-major, and we can say without asserting the identity of F#-major and Gb-major, that at the place marked they move in a kind of *balance*. Inner reasons, whose strength can already be recognized from the diagram and even more from the whole following narrative, plead for specially emphasizing the upper key F#-major, so that a larger semicircle of seven bright keys (above) is opposed to five dark or flat keys (below). These five dark keys lie beneath the horizontal line which divides the circle, whereas the two lying at the ends of this diameter itself (C and F#) belong to the upper semicircle (F# major still begins in the light, even though going down into the dark; on the other hand, F-major beginning certainly in the dark, surely ends in the light). Only with the minor keys which incline more to the dark, it is obvious for practical considerations to change D#-minor and G#-minor (the relatives of F#-major and B-major) enharmonically to Eb-minor and Ab-minor, so that these two minor keys fall within the circle of keys with flat notes. Thus for the minor keys a smaller semicircle of five bright keys and a larger semicircle of seven dark keys lie facing each other. The nature of the dark minor keys shows the preponderance of the dark circle (in Fig. 1, shaded darker). Likewise, the fact that Ab-minor and A-minor reach down into the dark corresponds to the nature of these keys. As in the major circle F#-major begins in the light and F-major ends in the light, so in the minor circle A-minor begins in the dark whereas Ab-minor is already in the dark.

The key of C-major, placed on the left end of the horizontal co-ordinate dividing the opposites of sharp and flat keys, is also the point of departure for accepted music theory. Like the key F#-major—whose tendency, inwardly considered, sinks—it occupies the transition point from above to below (the keys with flats), but its tendency, at the transition point from below to above, is to rise. Seen abstractly, the whole circle of keys can theoretically, of course, be drawn so that C-major would occupy any other position. The metaphysical reality, however, points to the *one* position.

As F#-major–G♭-major occupies the transition point from the sharp to the flat keys, so does C-major (with no key signature) occupy the transition point from keys with flat notes to those with sharp notes. The contrasting qualities of keys with sharp notes and keys with flat notes can be inwardly felt respectively as light and high, and then dark and deep. We feel something light and high with the keys with sharps, something dark and deep with the keys flat notes. (Such a general statement only becomes concrete when the individual nuances of each key are studied, as shall be attempted below.)

As this contrast of light, high and dark, deep is different with major and minor keys, we might add here that the sharp keys of the upper semicircle have a more strongly major quality with the minor quality appearing weaker, whereas the opposite prevails with the keys with flat notes: the minor quality is stronger and the major weaker. These things are already to be found expressed here and there in current music theory. This means, then, that the minor keys, in themselves dark and deep, appear on the lower side of the circle of keys as especially dark and especially marked in the minor character, whereas with the keys with sharp notes, inasmuch as they partake of a lighter character, the minor character appears weaker. On the other hand, the major keys in the upper sharp part of the circle of keys are particularly marked in their major character, whereas this undergoes a weakening in the darker flat keys of the circle. A-major is the key standing in the highest light facing C-minor, the one in the darkest depths, whereas C-major—A-minor (similarly with F#-major, too) forms a transition and a balance between light and dark, above and below.

As the horizontal co-ordinate C-major/A-minor–E♭-minor/F#-major (see Fig. 1) divides the circle of keys into a semicircle above of light and high keys from the dark and profound keys with flat notes below, so does the vertical co-ordinate A-major/F#-minor—C minor/E♭-major divide the circle into two halves which differ in a characteristic spiritual way. This no longer has to do with the opposites of dark and light, but with the direction of movement (indicated in Fig. 1 by the arrow). The direction of movement on the left-hand side of the semicircle of keys (E♭—C—A) is from below upwards, from dark to light, with the right hand (A—F#—E♭) the direction of movement is from above downwards, from light to dark. The keys on the left-hand semicircle reaching upwards to the light give the impression of a process of ever-brighter awakening, of consciousness becoming ever more outward; the keys on the right-hand side of the circle sinking downwards towards the dark, more the feeling of falling asleep or becoming dim, a continuous descent into the profound depths of inner consciousness. The keys of the rising semicircle: E♭-, B♭-, F-, C-, G- and D-majors are more matter-of-fact and clear; the keys of the falling semicircle: A-, E-, B-, F#-, D♭- and A♭-majors are more romantic and mystical. As C-major is the most pure and plain key, F#-major represents the romantic pole of the series of keys.

We come now to a survey of the individual keys and, in accordance with accepted music theory, we begin with C-major. We have already recognized the character of C-major with its ascending tendency as a transition from dark and depth to light and height, from that which is more within to that which is more outward and sense-oriented. All those composers who felt at all for the spiritual value of tonality[4]— and they can almost be graded according to how much they developed this feeling for the keys[5]—rightly recognized the character of C-major as a breakthrough of the light, a victory of light over darkness. The classic example of this is the transition from C-minor to C-major in Haydn's oratorio *The Creation* with the words from Genesis 'and there was light'. Or the powerful moment at the end of Weber's overture to *Freischütz* where, after the GP (which follows the development of the ravine and Samiel motifs created by the demonic weaving of the powers of darkness) a radiating C-major FORTISSIMO chord from the full orchestra announces the victory of the light, and leads over to the Agatha-motif with which the Overture ends, the motif of victorious love. In Wagner likewise, we find C-major to be the key that signifies the victory, above all in *Siegfried*, with Brünnhilde's awakening. (As all the keys of the rising part of the circle possess an awakening character, so usually C-major possesses the character of transition from dark to light.) With Beethoven, C-major strongly effects the breakthrough of light. In the *Fifth Symphony* he struggles through from the sombre, destiny-laden C-minor of the first movement to the radiant C-major of the Finale, here the breaking-out of victory over the dark forces of destiny (similarly with Bruckner's *Eighth Symphony* the contrast of the C-major Finale to the first movement in C-minor.) Mozart's *'Jupiter' Symphony* already allows us to feel this luminous, victorious key. In an especially majestic way we experience C-major as the 'breakthrough of the light' in the transition from B-major through C-major to the C#- minor Adagio in Bruckner's *Seventh Symphony* in E-major—'the breaking-in of a cosmic beam of light'.[6] 'The breakthrough of the light', this struggle from below upwards, from dark to light, gives the key of C-major in many ways the impression of willpower, of action. This character of will is touched upon in the effect of the broken C-major chord in the 'sword motif' in Wagner's *The Ring of the Nibelung*, of the

Mastersingers-theme and especially the C-major fanfare in the *Masters-ingers'* Prelude. (With Wagner, C-major is in quite a special sense 'the *Mastersingers*-key'.) Plenty of examples from all kinds of music show just this strength of will and the fanfare character of C-major. In other no less plentiful examples we feel C-major as the key of transition and balance between below and above, more as the neutral key, the key of clear, pure daylight. The classic example in this connection is Bach's C-major Prelude [*WTC* I], and similar pieces. In Act I of Wagner's *Parsifal*, C-major indicates the transition from the mystical darkness of the Grail (A-major) to the clear light of day.

As C-major is the breakthrough from below upwards, from dim to bright, from darkness to light, so in D-major (in the circle of fifths, the next key but one) we reach the utmost peak, penetrating through to the highest realms of light. Like C-major, D-major has something especially strong and positive; we feel, facing the force of will of C-major, more the light of thinking, of the spirit, in D-major. The key of D-major appears to belong especially to the Sun-filled spirit of J.S. Bach, the key in which he wrote many of his strongest movements. We need only point to the 'Sanctus' of the *B-minor Mass* and other similar movements of the great choral works, or to the D-major Fugue in Book I of *WTC*, which with its rhythmic penetration through to victory reminds us of the painting by Grünewald of the Resurrection. This character of D-major which attains the heights of light appears in Beethoven, for example in the great *Violin Concerto*. D-major appears to belong in a special way quite naturally to the violin and the string family in general which interprets the forces from above, the starry forces. D-major appears in its greatest intensity where Beethoven the symphonist at the end of his life's work, at the close of the Finale of the *Ninth Symphony* (D-minor), striving ecstatically reaches for the ultimate heights. In Wagner's *Parsifal*, the Parsifal-motif appears in Act I first as the motif of the young Parsifal, here in Bb-major; then, at the end of Act III where Parsifal wins through to the heights of the Grail kingdom, it leads up, so to speak, to his fulfilment in D-major. This is the key of 'attaining the ultimate heights' of spiritual light.

G-major stands more as a transition key between the strong keys of C-major, the breakthrough of the light, and D-major, reaching the heights of light. Although in classical music we find it used often enough, G-major as a leading tonic key has not the imposing contours of other keys, including the two mentioned above. Its true nature and worth comes out in more episodic use, in transition bars of a feeling nature and the like; in small, intimate pieces rather than in big symphonic works. Seen spiritually (for purely abstractly everything is just as equally possible, of course) it appears lighter and more natural to modulate to G-major, than from G-major to arrive at other keys. Between C-major with its strength of will and the thought-forces of D-major, G-major spans the middle region as the world of feeling. The deep soul-character of G-major comes to full expression in such passages of feeling as the episode in the Adagio of Beethoven's *Ninth Symphony*, or the *'Hammerklavier' Sonata* (op. 106), or the Trio from the third movement of Mozart's tenderly passionate *G-minor Symphony*, No. 39. The fullness of feeling of G-major intensifies the dreaminess of Schumann's *'Ich wandelte unter den Bäumen ...'*,[7] or especially in certain Musettes from Bach's Gavottes (e.g. the third *English Suite*), which so inimitably express the mood of quiet dreaming in the meadows. The world of feeling of a Haydn and Mozart is confided in a special way in G-major, and Schubert's *'Wohin?'* (*'Ich hört' ein Bächlein rauschen'*) and *'Haidenröslein'* appear to tell us of the most intimate secrets of this key. A certain effusiveness, a sparkling happiness full of rushing movement belongs to this key in Bach's Prelude and Fugue from *WTC* I. A strong inner awakening and hope for the light is eloquent in the G-major *'Wachet auf'* chorus in *Mastersingers*.

In A-major we reach those highest, radiant heights to which D-major was leading us. As D-major leads up to the highest peak, A-major contains the first step downwards which the arrow (see Fig. 1) indicates for the first time. A-major is the culmination of the movement upwards, and we might also say the turning point at the same time. Before the descent commences, however, we should realize that something like a zenithal pause occurs with A-major. A butterfly playing and hovering in the light, itself a creature of light, is perhaps the best picture from nature revealing the secrets of light in A-major. Grieg's poetic 'Butterfly' (from *Lyrical Pieces*, op. 43, no. 1) contains this inner meaning of A-major. A-major gains a certain inner quiet, a peaceful stillness in contrast to the dynamic nature of D-major: cf. the Larghetto from Beethoven's *Second Symphony*. Also in contrast to the clarity of thought in D-major, A-major as the first descending key shows the first touch of the romantic and mystical moods. Only a few of the greatest composers have really reached the ultimate spiritual heights of A-major. The delightful introduction to Beethoven's A-major *Seventh Symphony* conveys the zenithal pause in a charming romantic mood. And, if we follow Schwebsch (op. cit., p. 92), the first movement of Bruckner's *Sixth Symphony* in A-major is a resting in the spiritual heights which precedes the descent from this lofty experience, bringing it into the sphere of the everyday. Wagner reached the fullest and deepest secrets of A-major in *Lohengrin*, above all in the Prelude and in the Grail narration. A-major appears here the key pausing in the heights of the spiritual world from which the Grail journeys down to the earthly world. Nowhere in the whole of music is the key of A-major in its actual romantic and mystical character brought to such eloquent expression.

At this point, we should like to broaden our considerations which intend to examine the individual essence of each key, and try to gain an even more concrete picture. We found in the circle of keys a direction of movement which leads from darkness to light, and from the light down again into the dark. This rhythmic movement of the circle of the keys through all the changes of light and darkness finds its outer copy, suggested as though of itself, in each of the rhythmic movements of time through which the human being is led during the course of the day and of the year. This is not to be imagined as mere symbolism, but it does depend on whether or not we can spiritually experience each cycle of day and night, the light of summer and the darkness of winter. The whole consideration here over the question of the keys can only acquire meaning for those to whom the times of the day and the times of the year are not just abstract mathematical and astronomical statements, but who know how spiritually to experience morning and evening, midday and midnight, the heights of summer and the depths of winter, the months and the seasons. It is precisely our Christian festivals and seasons which appeal during the course of the year to such a spiritual participation.[8] When we have once recognized the inner relationship of the unity of the twelve keys with the spirit of the world, then we can find a meaning in its further relationships with space and time. If we can accordingly feel inwardly how Haydn in his oratorio *The Creation* musically expresses the transition from 'Let there be light' to 'and there was light' through a change from dark C-minor to C-major, the key of the rising light, the transition from darkness to light, then it is not far-fetched when we find for this C-major breakthrough of the light the immediate external picture of the sunrise. We do not remain, however, with the physical appearance of this sunrise, but in *inner experience* we find an immediate connection with that which we can inwardly feel and experience with the key of C-major. C-major has an inner connection to the hour of sunrise, and similarly its opposite, F#-major, to the hour of sunset (see Fig. 1).

We can experience the essence of the breakthrough of the light, which corresponds in the realm of the keys to C-major, still more intimately than with the external phenomenon of the sunrise during the course of the day. This is during the course of the year, at the point when the transition occurs from the dark half of the year towards the light. The time following the spring equinox, the time of Easter, the 'lighting up of the year' (this is the original meaning of the word *Ostern*—Easter—which viewed linguistically leads back to the same root as the words *Aurora, Eos,* and the Indian: *Uschas*). It is the season which corresponds to what we can inwardly experience with the key of C-major. (In order to achieve a spiritual view, it is good not to stick with only *one* picture, one external occurrence—as here the sunrise initially offered itself as the closest image from the world of the senses—but to grasp the linking and spiritually connecting element in the variety of images and sensory phenomena.) An experience which in this way does not remain with the crude, sensory aspect of phenomena, but points to the perceiving of what is inwardly expressed in the phenomena, we might call an 'occult experience'. It develops organs, for what remains hidden ('occult') for the purely external senses; [for this approach one might today prefer the term 'esoteric']. The spiritual science of earlier centuries created special signs to denote certain occurrences in the heavens and during the course of the year. For the experience of the time referred to above as 'the lighting up of the year' following the spring equinox, the traditional sign is the Ram ♈. It is well-known that the Sun does not stand at the time following the precise point of the equinox in the constellation of the Ram, but in the Fishes. We are nevertheless used to distinguishing the sign from the constellation, as does conventional astronomy as well. We speak of the sign of the Ram even when the Sun still stands in the *constellation* of the Fishes, and we mean the region of the ecliptic behind the separate signs of the zodiac which once centuries ago really did coincide with the constellation concerned. Today, however, they are already approximately one constellation removed.

It is necessary to note here, when in the following a 'sign of the [tropical] zodiac' is under discussion, not to confuse this sign with the constellation in which the Sun at the time concerned is to be observed [sidereal zodiac]. The spiritual science of earlier centuries employed the signs of the zodiac not as the expression of an external constellation or sign in the sky, but for a certain inner experience. Only in this purely spiritual sense, as an expression of such an experience, should they be taken in all the following observations. However distant such a system of signs may at first be for someone today, the justification for claiming this sign of the Ram ♈ for what lives in the key of C-major, lies in what has already been said about the connection of the spiritual during the course of the year to the circle of keys, before further light be shed from different points of view.

The concept of a twelvefold division of the year, which we shall now consider in its connection with the twelve keys, does not simply correspond to the twelve months. The mood of the time of year spoken of above is not our modern month of April, but the time which begins roughly between 20th and 24th of March, and ends between 20th and 24th April. In each month it is always these dates which mark the transition of the Sun to a new sign. The great changing points in the year, the solstices and equinoxes, fall at this time (we shall have to learn to approach these too from a certain spiritual point of view.) In the following considerations we shall simply for practical purposes name these measurements of time that are in question with the name of the month. The calendar month is not meant but the time from the last few days of the previous month when the sign changes, to a similar date in the month in questions.[9]

As the spiritual nature of C-major corresponds with the hour of sunrise in the course of the day, or with the lighting up of the year in the sign ♈, so we connect the spiritual nature of D-major which strives to the culminating height of the circle of keys, with the hour which ends with midday. The month in which the summer solstice and St John's Day occur is June (see the explanation above for this term). The Sun, and with it the year, strives to its height. The chosen sign for the spiritual experience meant here is the sign of the Twins, ♊. (At this time the Sun stands not in the Twins, but in the Bull.) Readers working inwardly in the right way on what has been said about D-major, when scanning the course of the year in their imagination, will find the connection as though of itself with the time when the year moves to its climax. As the character of D-major corresponds with the spirit of June, so the key of feeling, G-major, with its abundant urges and drives belongs spiritually to May, the time of year when nature blossoms and burgeons (at least in our latitudes) and appeals the strongest to the human soul and to human feelings. (Again, the calendar month is not meant here, but the time from about April 24th–May 24th.) In traditional esoteric language the sign of the Bull ♉ stands for this experience (the Sun nowadays stands at this time in the constellation of the Ram ♈).

In A-major the circle of keys reaches its climax, its culminating point (as is clear from the above observations) and at the same time the descent begins. The character of A-major corresponds in the course of the day to the character of the hour of midday, actually noon to 2 p.m. During the course of the year, if we can still feel intimately what is meant here, A-major would be the time of the summer solstice, the summit of the year and the following time of the first steps of descent. If we describe the character of A-major as a 'zenithal pause anticipating the descent', this agrees very much with what we experience purely externally during the course of the year. For as soon as the year turns from the heights of the Sun towards the dark, as soon as the days become markedly shorter, it stops for a few days at the heights it has reached *almost* standing still, moving on at first only slightly, unnoticeably. (For this reason, too: *solstitium*)—a similar resting point, this time in the depths, occurs at Christmas, around the Sun's winter solstice. As the circle of keys changes its direction of movement with A-major—the rising movement changes to a descent, which is obviously to be understood spiritually—so also does the Sun at this point in the year correspond spiritually with the key of A-major. In the esoteric sign-language which we have pointed to here, the change of direction at the zenith of a circular development is expressed through the sign of the Crab ♋. What hitherto was a rising movement, seen spatially, what was a forward direction (for the point of sunrise up here shifts in space further forward) now changes, and the movement continues further in reverse. In this connection the picture of the crab chosen for this sign-language is especially clear and understandable. (The external constellation, however, in which we have to seek the Sun nowadays, is not in the Crab but in that of the Twins. Nevertheless, conventional astronomy speaks here of 'the sign of the Crab').[10]

A-major, the culmination of the circle of keys, marks at the same time the beginning of the descent. The romantic character of the descending keys (in Fig. 1, the right-hand half following the arrow downwards) begins with A-major and appears stronger with the next key, E-major. On the other hand E-major can be felt as especially warm, indeed the warmest of all the keys. In older music, as in Bach—just to indicate here the *WTC*, especially the Prelude in Book I and the Fugue of Book II—suit the soul-warmth of E-major. We can also feel Beethoven's two E-major *Piano Sonatas*—both the quite early op. 14, no. 2 and the late op. 109—as outstanding 'warm' creations. Mendelssohn exploited the romanticism of E-major to an especial degree in his music to *A Midsummer Night's Dream*. In the *Songs Without Words*, too, we find this key especially close to his heart. Similarly, Schumann felt that his piece 'In Memory of F M' (*Album for the Young*, op. 68) should be heard in E-major. Bruckner, in his *Seventh Symphony* (especially the first and last movements) has brought to expression the romantic and warm nature of E-major to the highest degree. Schwebsch (op. cit.) called this symphony 'the greatest poem in E-major in music, all painted in blue over gold'. In contrast to the pure, cool character of the rising keys, those of the descending circle can be felt as 'poetic' keys. We noted above the contrast of the more vigorous, arousing character of the former keys and the restraining, suppressing character of the latter. Wagner uses E-major expressively for the romantic 'Sleeping-Beauty' ending to *The Valkyrie* (the sleep-motif of Brünnhilde). Equally characteristic is Schumann's 'Child Falling Asleep' from *Kinderscenen—Scenes from Childhood*, op. 15.

The spiritual position of E-major during the course of the day is early afternoon (two to four o'clock), when the light is subdued but the warmth is at its strongest, and in the year July–August (roughly 24th July–24th August), in which the light also becomes weaker, whereas the warmth as a rule reaches its highest intensity here in the year's decline. Thus E-major, the 'warmest' key ('warm' in the sense of soul-warmth) corresponds to this time of day and time of year when the warmth outside is usually at its height. The Sun stands here in the sign of the Lion—astronomically in the constellation of the Crab—and thus, remembering the earlier explanation, in the sign ♌, the esoteric expression of that spirituality which ensouls the key of E-major. The serene character of E-major, like the warmth, agrees with the serenity of this spirit, and also the serenity which can be experienced here in the time of day and of the year. The qualitative comparison of A-major and E-major, which have respectively more light and more warmth, agrees with the relationship outside with the time of day and of the year with which we connect the two keys.

If we feel with E-major especially warmth and fading light, then over the next key of the circle of fifths, B-major, something like *transfiguration* is spread, the transfigured and transfiguring gleam of the departing light. This would seem to us but seldom really expressively applied and only from the greatest composers. At the end of *Tristan* (Isolde's *Liebestod*—death for love), Wagner allows this transfigured and transfiguring nature of the key of B-major to speak to perfection. The ending of *Tristan and Isolde* shows the mightiest B-major in all music. B-major speaks expressively in the transfigured feeling and transfigured nature at the beginning of the *Karfreitagszauber*—the Good Friday magic, or 'Good Friday mood', in Wagner's *Parsifal*. This moves over to the bright, clarity of thought of D-major where the explanation by Gurnemanz spreads the light of thought over the transfiguration miracle experienced first through the feelings.[11] The sign of the Virgin in the Sun's yearly course connects the spirit of B-major with the time of year when we feel in the light of departing summer the approaching autumn. During the course of the day, this will be the hour before sunset, which experienced spiritually, corresponds to the mood of B-major. Wagner had the right feeling, too, in connecting the closing scene of *Tristan and Isolde* with the light of this hour.

We feel with B-major the hour which comes before sunset, or the time before the turn of the year in autumn, with their transfigured light. F#-major is the transition itself from the light into the dark. We experience this transition in the first place purely spiritually. We can say, however, that this spirituality can only be experienced in such outer images and processes as the sunset in the course of the day, and the pictorial expression of the turn of the year at autumn. This character of transition corresponds to the transcendental character of the key of F#-major. As the earthly daylight dies away little by little, the stars of the spiritual world begin in F#-major to light up. The delicate F#-major Trio in the Scherzo movement of Bruckner's *Ninth Symphony* speaks to us of such spiritual stars lighting up. The romantic-mystical nature of the descending keys intensifies here as far as the transcendental. As C-major is the 'cool pole' on the circle of keys, so F#-major (as noted in Chapter 4 above) is the opposite point from C-major (see Fig. 1), the romantic pole. The greatest masters of composition themselves have not often found their way as far as this transcendental quality of the key of F#-major. Bach uses this key expressively, as he does all the others, in the *WTC*, and Beethoven's tenderly felt F#-major *Piano Sonata*, op. 78, stands in the cycle near the point where he passes over from the epoch of the lofty heights in his output, to the mystical profundity of the late works.

Schumann, who leaned towards the 'chiaroscuro' and the transcendental quality of the dusk, of twilight in general, used the key of F#-major in many characteristic ways—especially in episodic passages of the greater piano works. In F#-major brightness is led into darkness; light and dark meet each other. The transition stretches here from the brighter keys with sharps to the darker ones with flats: the sharp keys coming from above, the flat keys from below. We can imagine (as noted above in Chapter 2) that here F#-major stands above facing Gb-major below, or that they meet at this transition point. That F#- major and Gb-major are not identical has already been emphasized enough. It can be said that both keys stand at this place to a certain extent in the balance. It is perhaps not without meaning that if we imagine the Sun's yearly course, we also meet on the corresponding place on the ecliptic the sign of the Scales ♎ (astronomically the Sun still stands during the time in question in the constellation of the Virgin ♍). It is the time after the autumn equinox when we enter the dark half of the year, when the days become shorter than the nights, the nights longer than the days. We can experience this time spiritually in different ways, either by looking towards the coming winter which approaches in the shortening days and the decline of the year—and this would be the feeling of G♭-major—or we enjoy the fading sunlight that just at this time of year continues in a certain evenness and in the surviving (though not for long) greenness of nature feel the last reflected splendour of the passing summer—and this would be the feeling of F#-major.

The transition from light to dark can also be seen as the transition from outer to inner, from a more sensory to a more spiritual sphere. Thus the keys which descend still further acquire an even more mystical character; the descent can be felt as a journey down into the profound depths of the inner world, the place of transition at F#-major as the 'threshold of the spiritual world'. Even more than with F#-major/G♭-major, we can feel with the solemn relative minor, E♭-minor. With no other key do we feel more expressively the proximity of the spiritual world and the way over to it, and no other master of sound has grasped more deeply this spiritual content of the key of E♭-minor than Bach in his E♭-minor Prelude from Book I of the *WTC*, the mood of which reminds us of the recitatives of Christ in the great Passions. It is the mood of Golgotha or Gethsemane that strikingly speaks to us in the solemn E♭-minor of this Prelude. In a more confused and obscure way Schumann brings to expression in his incidental music to *Manfred* the dread of the spiritual world in the key of E♭-minor. The E♭-minor opening of the Prelude to Wagner's *Twilight of the Gods* is also to be mentioned as characteristic in this connection.

Before further discussion on the dark keys with flats, it seems advisable to remain a while with the light keys with sharps (including C-major), and to cast a glance at their relative minors as well. As noted above, because of the predominance of the major character with these keys, it appeared inwardly appropriate to begin the discussion with the major keys. The relative-minor keys on this bright side of the circle of keys, inasmuch as they partake to a certain extent of the bright character of these keys, show the minor character only slightly. They give us more a toned-down feeling, a dimming of the light, when we allow them to work on us in imagination, like dull moments on a gloomy day. If C-major is the lighting up of the year in April, then A-minor would be standing between brightness and dimness, which just at this time is so frequently the mood of the daytime where light and dark, snow and sunshine, retreating winter and approaching spring struggle together ('April weather'). In the music of Mozart, A-minor produces a more soulful effect, like a 'smiling under tears', for example, the noble *Rondo* for piano (K. 511). In Grieg's music the pale, subdued light of the north frequently finds its striking expression in the key of A-minor (which Grieg has perhaps most intimately caught). From another point of view, A-minor shares the element of will with C-major—into which, through the minor mode, an expression of sombre resoluteness can easily be mixed. Here especially, the different A-minor Fugues of Bach can be recalled.

Similarly, E-minor has the element of feeling, of soul, in common with G-major, only this expression of feeling with the minor keys is more sombre, more plaintive, not infrequently more 'tearful'. Eastern Slavonic music—think of Russian folksongs and Tchaikovsky—appears especially suited to this elegiac key of E-minor. Chopin's unique manner comes to full expressive validity—think of the lamenting *Prelude* in E-minor [op. 28, no. 4], perhaps the most intensive soul-expression of weeping in the whole of music. This lamenting feeling of E-minor is intensified to a sublime, cosmic grandeur with Bach in the 'Crucifixus' from the *B-minor Mass*. B-minor itself, the relative of D-major, is the intense opposite of D-major, above all as Klingsor's key in Wagner's *Parsifal*. Like D-major, B-minor is also spiritual, but with the adverse thoughts of the dark adversary. As Parsifal reaches the heights in D-major and becomes the Grail King, so Klingsor wants to take by storm the (for him) unassailable heights of the Grail, with his adverse thoughts in B-minor. In other cases, the character of B-minor is more elegiac, or something lies within it which disposes us to serious contemplation. Bach chose this key for the great cosmic subject of the sacrifice of the Mass.

F#-minor can have either a more elegiac effect, as in the F#-minor Prelude from Book II of the *WTC*, or it appears as the exact opposite of A-major and its illumined heights. It is just the spiritually exalted plane of A-major which allows the minor opposite to be felt possibly as the 'abyss'. We find a classic example of F#-minor used as the 'key of the abyss' in Weber's *Freischütz*, in the ravine music. There the characteristic shrill piping of the piccolos ('*Milch des Mondes fiel aufs Kraut*') reminds us at the same time of the connection which F#-minor has to the heights of A-major and gives this minor key a peculiarly ardent nuance. We feel a deep 'abyss of suffering' in the F#-minor Adagio from Beethoven's great '*Hammerklavier*' *Sonata*, op. 106.

As E-major speaks to us romantically of summer days, or summer nights too (as Mendelssohn's *Midsummer Night's Dream*), so quite especially does the relative C#-minor tell of the night of summer and the romantic light of the Moon. Music critics like [Adolf Bernhard] Marx [1795-1866] censure the name '*Moonlight Sonata*' which is applied to Beethoven's op. 27, no. 2, because it did not originate from Beethoven himself and because the sonata 'has nothing to do with moonlight'. In reality a more appropriate name for this elegiac sonata, which is pure Beethoven and is full of longing, could never have been found. In its characteristic key of C#-minor, there lives and weaves everything which we can feel, spiritually experienced, in connection with the Moon romanticism and longing. Bruckner intensifies the key of C#-minor to its greatest expression in the Adagio from his *Seventh Symphony*, which Schwebsch (op. cit.) calls 'the great prayer to the night'. Bach too connects the expression of soul-warmth with this key to a special degree (see the Preludes and Fugues of the *WTC*). As D#-minor, the relative of F#-major, lies further from us than the enharmonically-related Eb-minor (see above), so similarly does G#-minor, the relative minor of B-major. We feel Ab-minor as more fully expressive and to an extent a more natural key, which through its key signature moves over to the sphere of the keys with flats reaching down to their profound depths. When purely formally it is not the actual relative of B-major, it can nevertheless be inwardly so perceived (the minor character of itself tends more to keys with flats—see above, end of Chapter 2). Just as B-major speaks to us in a certain way of the separation of the light, so we feel with A♭-minor the most painful mood of farewell, a farewell to daylight, the light of life. This character of the key of A♭-minor reaches its deepest level with Beethoven in the A♭-minor Arioso from the A♭-major *Piano Sonata*, op. 110, which already at its opening is filled with a certain mood of farewell. The spiritual character of the key of E♭-minor has already been discussed above (p. 27).

The circle of keys leads us deeper into the realms of the dark keys with flats from the point of transition marked by F#-major/ G♭-major and E♭-minor. It is here that the minor keys in particular show most strongly the dark character, whereas the major keys, which are brighter, are diminished through this dark area of tonality.

From the region of the Scales (F#/G♭-majors, E♭-minor) we reach the Scorpion ♏, in whose sign the year or the summertime of the year experiences at the same time the sting of death. This spiritual region, which in the course of the year corresponds to the time from the end of October to near the end of November, in the course of the day is the real fall of night following the dusk. The dark, destructive element which streams out from the spirit of this sign, the being and effect of the might of death, is most immediately expressed in the key of B♭-minor. Wagner uses it in *Twilight of the Gods* (especially in Act II) as the key for the wielding of the powers of darkness, the key of Hagen-Alberich. Bach's B♭-minor Prelude (*WTC*, Book I) conveys more a noble mood of the Passion, the mood of the fulfilment of the Crucifixion. Here and there B♭-minor appears as the key of death; an expressive example is Chopin's *Funeral March* (as in the whole B♭-minor *Piano Sonata*, op. 35). In D♭-major, the relative major, we experience something brighter, a light that is kindled in the dark depths within when the outer light is extinguished. When we look out of doors, the D♭-feeling can waken in us when the sunlight falls on the last fallen leaves. D♭-major, as the key of Chopin's *Nocturnes*, speaks of penetrating to the secret depths within. Somewhat grander than Chopin, Bruckner in the Adagio of the *Seventh Symphony* knew how 'to fill the widths and depths of the soul-depths of D♭-major'.[12] A deep experience of consecration sounds in D♭-major, as similarly from the D♭-major passage in the Adagio of Beethoven's *Ninth Symphony*. D♭-major becomes there the key of consecration, the priestly key, which speaks of the most sacred inner human depths. In a somewhat different way Beethoven leads us in the D♭-major Andante of the *'Appassionata' Sonata* (op. 57) into inner, dark depths. We can feel this movement as a prayer, a cry out of the depths.

The key A♭-major/F-minor leads us to still darker depths. If B♭-minor expresses a darkening or a dying, then F-minor goes even further.

Here it is positively night, and the direction of movement of F-minor which leads us right down to the furthest depths, is from darkness to deepest dark. No other key, not even C-minor, is so sombre as F-minor. For C-minor standing at the deepest point on the circle of keys nevertheless bears the upward movement and with it a moment of brightening up. It seems worth noting that the Sun-filled Bach himself when he wrote in F-minor, fell into a certain gloominess and darkening (as in the *WTC* or any of the other small F-minor pieces). F-minor is the key of the night which becomes ever darker, up to midnight. Rightly and expressively Schumann's 'In the Night' (*Phantasiestücke*, op. 12, no. 5) is consequently written in F-minor. In the first movement of Bruckner's *Ninth Symphony* we experience most intensely the nocturnal darkness of F-minor. Towards the end, after stars delicately light up over a mystical-flickering chord (G#, D, E, F#, B), after shorter and even grander modulation through a long passage, sustained by the full orchestral fff, the full darkness is finally victorious in an F-minor, sounding ppp, and a black veil, dark as night, is spread over the world. The colour black is most intensively represented in this F-minor from Bruckner's *Ninth Symphony*.

In F-minor we can especially sense this passionate soul-quality of the night. Beethoven's *'Appassionata' Sonata* (op. 57) stands before us as the most mighty expression of this side of F-minor. The *Sonata Pathetique* (op. 13) in C-minor is also passionate, but here, as in Bruckner's C-minor *Eighth Symphony* filled with passion, we find an upward-striving which could lead beyond this (and Bruckner does indeed achieve it). In Beethoven's *'Appassionata' Sonata*, however, the dark night of passion completely dominates, from which the soul finds no release. This darkness without light, in which no ray of hope breaks, finds in F-minor its most telling expression.

The connection of this key to the relative Ab-major is similar to the relationship already established between Bb-minor and Db-major. F-minor in comparison to Bb-minor leads to even greater darkness, as does Ab-major compared to Db-major lead to even more mystical depths within. As F-minor is the most gloomy key, so the relative Ab-major is the most mystical of all the keys. Whereas F-minor only contains darkness, Ab-major contains 'the light that shines in the darkness'. This light is kindled first and shines brightest when all external light is extinguished. In this key we are furthest away from daily life and the everyday consciousness. Whereas Eb-major, the next key on the circle of fifths, takes the upwards direction once more to a new awakening, Ab-major leads us still deeper into the inner realm.

Many musical examples from Bach, Beethoven (*Piano Sonatas* op. 26 and 110, Adagio from the *Fifth Symphony*), Schubert and many others demonstrate the character of this key. Wagner, the musical mystic par excellence has fathomed most deeply and inimitably the mystical nature of this key. We find outstanding use of Ab-major in the duet from *Tristan and Isolde*, in the great nocturnal scene in Act II, 'O sink hernieder, Nacht der Liebe', and in *Parsifal* (Prelude, Grail celebration in Act I, and end of Act III). If the Mysteries of night and love are present in *Tristan & Isolde*, which is where the mysticism of Ab-major leads us, in *Parsifal* it is the Christ-Mystery itself carried by the 'I', the crimson glowing Grail, the flowing blood from the wounds on Golgotha. Ab-major is the key of the glowing Grail, and, as previously noted, after covering up the light of the Grail, C-major arrives as the key of the reappearing bright day. For knowledge of the spiritual character of tonality, we can draw especially upon *Parsifal* for deep revelations.

During the course of the day, the hours before midnight correspond to the spiritual region of the keys of F-minor and Ab-major, and in the course of the year to the time leading to Christmas, the time of the year's deepest darkness when the already long nights become longer still and the days still shorter and darker. The esoteric sign for the spirit of this epoch in the Sun's course and of the year, is the Archer ♐. With this sign we connect musically the spirituality of F-minor/Ab-major. We think more of the darkness of the year with F-minor; with Ab-major more of the mystic mood of Advent. We inwardly anticipate the rekindling of the light of Christmas, the light that shines in the darkness.

This Christmas light itself, proclaiming to us that it is now moving again towards the light of awakening, comes to its musical expression in E♭-major. The upwards direction of the arrow (see Fig. 1) suits this key, joining it to the family of cooler, clearer keys on the left-hand semicircle which make for awakening and the light. As the meaning of A-major is a zenithal pause (before the first descending movement), so E♭-major, the opposite pole from A-major, means a 'pause at the nadir', before the first upward movement. As Wagner's Prelude to *Lohengrin* similarly expresses the zenithal pause that belongs to A-major, so his Prelude to *Rheingold* does the same for the resting point at the nadir that belongs to E♭-major. In the former it is the Grail resting in the heights of light of the spiritual world before it descends to Earth; in the latter it is the gold treasure reposing in the depths of the Rhine, and the surge of the Rhine itself in the depths. Nowhere else in music do we remain for so long in a single key, one keynote and tonic chord, and in no other key could we rest as in E♭-major. Schumann uses E♭-major and the relative C-minor for his Lieder concerning the depths of the Rhine. We find this pause at the nadir in the Sun's yearly course at the time of the winter solstice around Christmas, when for a few days the increase in the light remains almost unnoticeable. The spirituality of this time—which can be experienced more than any other—is ruled over and expressed by the sign of Capricorn ♑ (today the Sun at this time is in the constellation of the Archer ♐). It is the same spirituality which we find again musically in the keys of E♭-major and C-minor. With C-minor we feel more the darkness and the depths of the year, with E♭-major, the kindling of the Christmas light. With Bach this Christmas mood sounds in an especially warm way in the E♭-Prelude of the *WTC* Book II.

Because the turning from below to above, from dark to light, happens in them, E♭-major and C-minor appear as especially strong keys (for example, essentially stronger than the opposite pole A-major/F#-minor) and thus in music they are preferred for large-scale movements, for works in the grand style: Beethoven's *'Eroica' Symphony* (E♭-major) and *Fifth Symphony* (C-minor). The upward striving, upward struggling that is present in the key of E♭-major (as in the spirit of the corresponding time of year) is especially shown as the key of struggling heroes—as D-major is that of victorious heroes (cf. also the E♭-major episode in Beethoven's *Piano Sonata*, op. 106, first movement). The dark C-minor is the special key of tragic warrior heroes. Beethoven's *Fifth Symphony* as well as Bruckner's 'Michaelic' *Eighth Symphony* show in different ways, though both in immense contexts, the hero's struggle 'from the night to the light' (C-minor–C-major). The C-minor *Funeral March* in the 'Eroica' portrays the tragedy of the hero's life. C-minor is the tragic hero's key in Wagner, too: the Funeral Music on Siegfried's death in *Twilight of the Gods*, with the Siegfried-motif and the Volsungs-motif in C-minor. This key, with all its tragic seriousness and despite its spiritual depth is less sombre than F-minor, because it carries the upward movement within itself. In C-minor, the struggle is taken up that leads to the victory in C-major. This is the content of Beethoven's last *Piano Sonata*, op. 111, in two movements, expressed in an especially intimate and spiritual way. It can be experienced as an upwards struggle out of the Earth's night to the light of higher worlds. C-minor and E♭-major initiate the first movement towards the light, to C-major, the victory of the light. With each of the two following keys on the circle of fifths, we draw nearer to this victory of the light. We experience this nearness, however, substantially more with the major keys than with the relative minors. Where we can put greater emphasis on the minor keys leading downwards on the dark semicircle, to get to know properly the nature of those rising, we should keep in mind the major keys (E♭, B♭, and F).

Compared with E♭-major, the next key on the circle of fifths, B♭-major, is already a stage nearer the rising of the light. We can associate the feeling of B♭-major with what we spiritually experience when in the dark the light makes its first appearance, when in winter the first divining of spring is announced. We have moved from the sign of Capricorn to that of the Waterman occupied by the Sun from the end of January to the end of February (in the sky today the Sun stands in Capricorn).

It is the time when not infrequently the first sunny days announce the coming of spring. It might be recalled how Wagner in *The Valkyrie* sets his '*Winterstürme wichen dem Wonnemond*' in B♭-major. This has to do not with the real delight of spring but with the still deceptive anticipation of spring. Schumann's music especially gives us the chance to experience this delicate hope of spring in different nuances, as well as that other mood of this key between light and dark which we call 'chiaroscuro'. It is the mood of the light which surrounds us when we step out of the glaring sunlight of day into the twilight darkness of a deep pine forest. Consequently, in Schumann's *Woodland Scenes*, op. 82, the 'Entrance to the Wood' is written expressively in B♭-major, as are other pieces in the set ('Lonely Flowers', 'Pleasant Landscape', 'Farewell').

B♭-major in Wagner's *Parsifal* appears first in the motif of the young hero. In the soul's realm a certain basis of hope and trust is linked with B♭-major, with which in a strong characteristic way Bach's B♭-Fugue (*WTC* I) is imbued. We feel in Bach's use of B♭-major a quiet and sure assurance of faith. But with some of Beethoven's works—think of the great B♭-major 'Hammerklavier' Sonata, op. 106—we feel a titanic storming of bold hope, which, however, is broken off by destiny, until finally only an empty abstraction of that strong feeling remains (the closing Fugue). Beethoven's *Fourth Symphony* occasionally recalls Schumann through the peculiar twilight 'chiaroscuro' characteristic of B♭-major.

If with B♭-major we already sense the light within the darkness, with the relative G-minor it is still predominantly the darkness that we feel. If B♭-major is perhaps premature hope as far as the soul is concerned, then perhaps G-minor is a premature abandoning of all hope (cf. Pamina's G-minor lament in Mozart's *The Magic Flute*). Mozart's *G-minor Symphony* No. 39 is borne throughout by a passionate feeling of suffering which can gain no proper light of consolation. Bach has left us powerful and monumental compositions in G-minor of predominantly sombre character. We can feel that it is characteristic of G-minor that Bach should permit the tragic and serious G-minor Fugue (*WTC* I) to end in an uninterrupted, tragic G-minor without this gleam of hope. Bach otherwise preferred to conclude his movements in minor keys with a shimmer of hope in the major.[13]

As B♭-major shows us the first announcement of the light in the darkness, the next key on the circle of fifths, F-major, comes immediately before the dawning of the light. F-major in a certain way shares the brightness of C-major, just as the Sun's brightness in the pre-dawn of morning already illuminates the world before its rising, or as sunny March days before the actual equinox announce the coming of spring, the lighting up of the year. On the other hand, by still belonging to the lower sphere of keys, F-major appears as more inward, intimate and heartfelt than C-major. The light, as external light, is not yet so strong as with C-major, but is felt more as a spiritual light. As the hour before sunrise has a special inwardness and its light a certain sanctity, so does the key of F-major carry with it as one of its possibilities this mood of sanctity, of holiness. F-major consequently offers itself especially for religion, the key for hymns:[14] the tune *'Wie schön leuchtet der Morgenstern'* sounds most naturally in F-major, even appears as though wanting to reveal something of the nature of the key of F-major itself. The feeling of hallowed devotion also sounds in the F-major of Beethoven's *Pastoral Symphony*. Apart from the pastoral element, for which Bach and others have chosen F-major, it also includes humour—similarly, the other F-major symphony, the *Eighth Symphony*. However different religious and humorous moods are in other connections, they have one thing in common, that we lift ourselves in both moods above the outer world to overcome the weight of external things. This rising above mundane things is a mark of F-major in contrast to the otherwise spiritually-akin C-major. Above all lightness, grace, suits the key of F-major, and with Bach it is revealed in the Fugue-form—listen to the light-bathed, humorous charm of the F-major Fugue of *WTC* II. With Beethoven we find this light charm, this maidenly quality in the F-major *Piano Sonata*, op. 10, no. 2, in which humour breaks through in the last movement.

In contrast to the more masculine C-major or D-major, F-major has a feminine or maidenly element in it, as does G-major in another way. Something of the light, comfortable ease of the flowing waves lives in F-major. Think not only of 'Scenes by the Brook' in Beethoven's *Pastoral Symphony No. 6*,[15] but especially of Schubert's *'Trout'* Quintet, characteristic of F-major to the highest degree.

F-major is the key which joins the lower darker keys with the higher brighter ones, combining the inner with the outer, the spiritual with the physical, external light with the spiritual light. Consequently, F-major is above all the key of sublimated feeling for nature, too, for which Beethoven's *Pastoral Symphony* is the unsurpassable classic example.

It is said—and the truth of this observation cannot be attested here—that F is the actual basic note in the weaving of nature, of all natural sounds in general: the rippling of the brook the sighing of the wind, indeed F-major (or rather the note F) lies behind the very roar of a distant city. If this is correct, a musical complement would offer itself to what could be said more in linguistic terms about the primal sound and the sound of nature.[16] F-major, the 'key of the earth', unites a feeling for nature with a feeling for religion. Thus when we seek again the spiritual connection of the circle of keys with the yearly course of the Sun, the time of year at which we arrive, the time of fasting preceding Easter (the end of February to the end of March), unites an intimate religious feeling with an awakened feeling for nature in people's spiritual experience. In the language of the signs of the zodiac, which we have drawn on in this essay, the spirituality meant here finds its expression in the sign of the Fishes ♓. (The constellation in the heavens at this time which the Sun occupies nowadays is the Waterman ♒; it enters the Fishes today roughly at the spring equinox.) People always felt the uniting of the cosmic-spiritual element with the earthly-physical element as a special religious meaning of this sign.

Moving on from here, a little light can perhaps be shed on the secrets of the key of D-minor, the relative minor of F-major, to which we should now proceed to complete our observations. It is the last minor key still lying completely in the dark, taking no share in the glimmer of light from above, which already falls on its relative major. The contrast between the major key and its relative minor can be felt especially strongly here. Whereas we already experience in F-major the light of the approaching Resurrection morning, D-minor allows us to experience something like the darkness of the grave, the rigid, stony tomb. It is the gloomy mood of burial which in the days of the year described here we can very frequently experience, too, when in a time whose approach we long for the spring, nature lies still dark and sombre before our eyes, cold winds shake the naked boughs of the trees and winter numbness seems unwilling to relent. It is that mood of the year which brings in its wake the spiritual-religious experiences of the Passion, Good Friday and Easter Saturday. The mood of such days felt at this time of year could not only be expressed through F-major or be brought into a connection with it. Their spirit finds much rather a musical correspondence in D-minor.

Bach, Beethoven, Wagner, Bruckner and many others help us to feel in the key of D-minor this rigid, stony character of the tomb (here we recall the passage with the 'stony guest' in Mozart's *Don Giovanni*, which is also written in D-minor). The D-minor movements of Bach (e.g. in the *WTC*) show this mood, still more Beethoven's D-minor *Piano Sonata*, op. 31, no. 2. Then, above all, the first movement of Beethoven's *Ninth Symphony* which in sombreness, far from the life-inspiring processes of the Sun, places us into a gloomy cosmic loneliness. Chopin's unique 'stony' D-minor *Prelude* should be mentioned. The most tremendous elaboration of the stony character of the grave, of the tomb, of the key of D-minor, is worked out in Bruckner's *Ninth Symphony*. It leads us in the introduction, and still more tremendously and shatteringly at the end of the first movement, to the sublime, divine, majestic Fatherhood of Death, the great *mysterium tremendum*. Schubert speaks to us tenderly, amiably but still spiritually aware of this direction, in his immortal *D-minor String Quartet 'Death and the Maiden'* (after the song of the same name). The name and the whole musical language of this quartet interprets an unfathomably profound spiritual meaning in the whole contrast of D-minor and F-major.

The circle of fifths of the system of keys leads up from D-minor/F-major back to our point of departure in C-major, the resurrection of the light.

Postscript[17]

Naturally enough, examples of the spiritual character of the keys should be taken from well-known classical music. It does not follow from this that the subject has meaning only for this music from the past. Meaning is also obtained especially for music of the future—even if this music should be unlike earlier music which rests in tonality—when it combines in the freest manner the colours and nuances of individual keys. Very much depends on how keys are combined or passed through, whether the result is to feature the right colour-nuance. The right key, however, will only be found if composers have the right concepts of the spiritual character and value of the individual keys. The great masters of the past had a certain instinctive sense for this. But in the future it will become increasingly necessary consciously to lay hold of the spiritual nature of tonality, if the feeling for keys is not to become lost.

Some Further Reading[18]

Hermann Beckh: *Die Sprache der Tonart: Von Bach bis Bruckner*, Urachhaus, Stuttgart 1999 / Fischer Taschenbücher 1987. Eng. tr. *The Language of Tonality: Music from Bach to Bruckner*, tr. A.S. Anastasi 2015, rev. ed. Temple Lodge.

Beckh's thesis on tonality is acknowledged by two subsequent researchers who each devote a chapter to summarize it:

Christoph Peter, *Die Sprache der Musik in Mozarts Zauberflöte*, Verlag Freies Geistesleben, Stuttgart 1997, pp. 130-142. Eng. tr. A.S. *The Language of Music in Mozart's The Magic Flute*, Anastasi 2014, pp. 173-88. Re-issue: TL forthcoming.

Heiner Ruland: *Ein Weg zur Erweiterung des Tonerlebens*. Verlag Die Pforte, Basel 1981. pp. 54-60. Eng. tr. *Expanding Tonal Awareness: A Musical Exploration of the Evolution of Consciousness*, Rudolf Steiner Press, Forest Row 2014.

Further insights regarding the tonal system, see the collected essays of Prof. Pfrogner, in particular:

Hermann Pfrogner: 'Hat Diatonik Zukunft?', in *Zeitwende der Musik*, Lange Müller, München/ Wien 1986, pp. 268-92. Eng. tr. A.S. in MS, 'Has the diatonic system a future?'

A further full-length study:

Friedrich Oberkogler, *Tierkreis- und Planetenkräfte in der Musik: Vom Geistgehalt der Tonarten*, Novalis Verlag, Schaffhausen 1987.

The Parsifal=
Christ=Experience

Hermann Beckh

Part 2

THE PARSIFAL =
CHRIST=EXPERIENCE
in
Wagner's Music Drama

Translator's Preface

In 1891, Hermann Beckh, then sixteen-years-old, visited Bayreuth for his first experience of Wagner's final music drama *Parsifal*. It was decisive for his whole life; he always referred to it in the warmest terms. Not only the story but the music pointed to a Christian path of knowledge, a 'pathway to the Holy Grail' independent of ecclesiastical confessions. Beckh felt drawn to a non-sectarian Christianity as a distinct possibility, also transcending national boundaries. In his memoirs, he writes:

> Something [in me] wanted to reach this experience of humanity but had not yet come through … But this is exactly the situation of young Parsifal in Act 1, who also stands before the wonder of the Grail, sees the suffering Amfortas and in him the whole pain of humanity … [N]ot only did the dramatic content of the play lay hold of me, also the music shook me; already the A♭-major of the Prelude made a deep impact on my young soul [*Hermann Beckh: Life and Work*, TL 2021, p. 57].

In point of fact, Beckh maintained *Tristan and Isolde* was the supreme musical experience of his life—the major work discussed in *The Mystery of Musical Creativity* (TL 2019). But he also recognized that without writing that music drama, Wagner would not have been able to tackle *Parsifal*, from which task the composer initially recoiled (letter to Mathilde Wesendonck, 1859). One important link is the use of the key of A♭-major in both music dramas.

> Purely musically, the genius of Wagner was able to create *Tristan and Isolde* as most beautiful and complete. However, before the entrance portal to the Christian Mystery, the story of Tristan and the music of *Tristan and Isolde* remain standing still full of longing. Yet it is important to establish that a *way* leads from *Tristan* the A♭-major to the *Parsifal* A♭-major. Without this *Tristan* A♭-major, the *Parsifal* A♭-major could never have been created [*The Language of Tonality*, 239].

Beckh identified with the theme of longing, of suffering, having experienced in a spontaneous vision already as a five-year-old in the mountains that pre-natal existence was a reality. The experience returned during his student years in Munich, strongly reminding him of his destiny to help humanity, eventually finding tangible form in his ordination as a founder-priest of The Christian Community, a movement for religious renewal. This event he experienced as the goal of his striving. In the appreciation Emil Bock wrote during the last year of his life (1959), he records:

> He had always longed that the Logos, driven to abstraction in our time, wants to resurrect in its full creative and healing power. To celebrate the spirit-word in the Service at the new altars was really the innermost fulfilment of this particular destiny. Beckh himself was always amazed at the enigmatic straight-forwardness with which, despite all apparent detours and confusion, his angel had led him to this goal [*The Language of the Stars*, 501].

The present translation made with Anneruth Strauss was completed in 1988. It appeared in 2014, some twenty-six years on, needing slight editing with an updated bibliography and notes. With further slight editing, it reappears today during the Centenary year of The Christian Community, 2022.

The interested reader will find much in Friedrich Oberkogler, *Richard Wagner vom Ring zum Gral*, Stuttgart, Verlag Freies Geistesleben 1985². The section on *Parsifal* was issued separately, *Parsifal: Der Zukunftsweg des Menschen in Richard Wagners Musikdrama*, Stuttgart, Verlag Freies Geistesleben 1983. It is curious that this genial and prolific author fails adequately to acknowledge his obvious debt to Beckh's pioneer work, but there again one unfortunately repeatedly meets that phenomenon.

My thanks to Neil Franklin for his habitual helpful advice. All remaining blemishes in this edition are due to my oversights.

Alan Stott
All Souls' 2021

Introduction
Richard Wagner and Christianity[19]

On 13th February 1883, when he was not yet seventy-years-old, Richard Wagner, creator of the new music drama, died in Venice, in the Palazzo Vendramin, the very place where he had completed Act II of *Tristan and Isolde*, that great work of art that was so dear to his heart.

We shall now attempt an estimate of Wagner, not from the musical point of view but simply in his significance for Christianity. We know how near he came at the end of his life's work, in *Parsifal*, to the deepest Christian truths, those of a spiritual Christianity. Such truths had already been dimly perceived in the Parsival legends of the Middle Ages in the legend of the Holy Grail, and today through anthroposophy they have been made fully accessible to human perception. Rudolf Steiner emphasized this distinctly in one of his Easter lectures in Berlin, when he spoke of the 'secrets of the Blood of Golgotha'.

Wagner was actually the first in our age to give expression to the way in which Christ's Deed, which changed the whole Earth, is connected with the secrets of the blood. This is the Mystery of the Holy Grail, which has strongly affected a wide group of people because it was not only conveyed intellectually in words, but was supported by music which flows into the soul with almost magical power. And, as Steiner once said, of all the arts people today are most receptive to music. Yet for the evolution of our age it is most important that understanding should come through thinking perception rather than through dim feeling.

Indeed, the Mystery of Golgotha, the secret of the Blood of the Holy Grail, which finds its ritual expression in the cup of the Last Supper as given in the Mass and the Act of Consecration of Man of The Christian Community, a movement for religious renewal, has shone powerfully into Wagner's musical and dramatic work. This was already the case in the work of his middle life, in *Lohengrin* (completed 1848); in *Parsifal* this tremendous Mystery is the central matter.

Yet these two music dramas of the Grail by no means exhaust Wagner's significance for Christianity. It is especially characteristic of Wagner that for him the Christian Mystery ultimately emerged from earlier cycles of myths and mysteries, from the Teutonic *Ring of the Niebelung* and the Celtic *Tristan and Isolde*. This gives to his Christianity the slant that humanity is longing for more or less consciously today, distinguishing it from ecclesiastical Christianity. Christ Himself speaks to the disciples of such a Christianity of the future (John 16:12), and John the Evangelist, too (John 20:31; 21:25, the very last verse). In later times it is spoken of above all by Novalis, who is so deeply penetrated by the Johannine spirit: 'There is no religion that would not be Christianity.' 'In the gospels lie the fundamentals of future and higher gospels.' 'Christianity must be studied for eternities. It then grows ever loftier, richer and more magnificent.'

Just because the Christian element in Wagner is built up from pre-Christian ('pagan') primary sources it consequently appears so profound, wide and deep, so world-embracing. We learn there to form quite different ideas about 'paganism' and its relationship to Christianity from those that are still common in many circles. Those who can realize the unity of the inner development in Wagner's life-work will find themselves considerably helped by this to understand a worldwide Christianity. And it may well be said that among the great in art and literature, not even excepting Goethe, there are only a few whose work has been so highly unified and complete as the life-work of Richard Wagner. Let us consider his work under this aspect and that of Christianity.

Deeply impressionable as he was in his childhood for all that has to do with religion and ritual, Wagner in his later life was certainly not a pious church-goer. This does not prevent our meeting in his works with the ecclesiastical externals of Christianity. *The Mastersingers* begins with a scene in church with solemn hymns, during which Eva, a member of the singing congregation, exchanges looks of love with the youthful Walter Stoltzing as he stands watching. To Wagner, who created musically in *Tristan and Isolde* a sublime 'starry cathedral' for the Mystery of love, there was nothing wrong in this. In *Lohengrin*, Act II, we find a procession going to church with organ music, Lohengrin's wedding procession with Elsa. In *Rienzi*, too, with the scene set in the Rome of the Middle Ages, we meet with Catholic rituals. Similarly, in *Tannhäuser* there is the 'Pilgrims' Chorus'. It is well-known that in the part of this drama which deals with Tannhäuser's experiences in Rome, the head of the Catholic Church does not appear in a favourable light.

All this shows that Wagner did not simply pass over that which is Christian. Even if at first we look superficially, we find that he passed it by less even than Goethe, who has given us so much that makes for higher things, for the 'Mysteries of Christianity'—to use a phrase of Novalis. In Wagner, the bridge between ecclesiastical and super-ecclesiastical Christianity is more apparent and more easily felt than in Goethe. With what cosmic depths of insight he could experience the Christian ritual—the Eucharistic sacrifice—is shown by the Grail celebration in *Parsifal*. In *Parsifal*, the church, or better the temple, as the Grail Temple, is really an *image* of the cosmic Starry Temple that we find in *Tristan and Isolde*, and the Temple of Humanity at which we guess, distantly at least, in *The Mastersingers*. And Wagner, like Bruckner, has actually adopted individual elements from church music, especially chorales, or hymns, as the chorale in *The Mastersingers* and the 'Faith-Motif' in *Parsifal*. We find these elements of church music also in *Rienzi, The Flying Dutchman, Tannhäuser* and *Lohengrin*.

A deeper Christian perspective in Wagner's work is found already in his early opera *Die Feen* ('The Fairies')—which does not yet show the real Wagnerian style. Certain clearly-marked motifs are present, derived from the mysteries but not yet decidedly Christian. They could probably be more easily pointed out in *The Flying Dutchman*, especially in the secret of its final apotheosis. But it is only from *Tristan and Isolde* onwards that this becomes clearer. *Tristan*, in spite of the very different level of maturity, has much in common with *The Flying Dutchman*, even musically. The latter seems spiritually still to lie in an Indian, Buddhistic realm, within the conceptual sphere of Sansara and Nirvana; that is to say, the cycle of repeated earth-lives and ultimate release. Only in *Parsifal* do we see more distinctly 'repeated earth-lives' raised into a Christian sphere.[20]

Wagner's next opera, *Tannhäuser*, youthfully unripe in many respects, in other respects highly original, is extremely important when considered in connection with both facets of Christianity. At its heart is the Mystery of St Elizabeth. A superficial judgement finds here that Wagner has done violence to history. Elizabeth, the young wife of Count Ludwig of Thuringia, daughter-in-law of Count Hermann, has become the maiden niece of Count Hermann; Elizabeth's death occurred quite differently, and also happened in another place (not, as in Wagner's opera, in the surroundings of the Wartburg). And yet such a one-sided emphasis on external history would wrong Wagner in a deeper sense. For here, as well as elsewhere, Wagner does not *want* to bring out the merely historical fact, but to express in pictures the deeper relationships that are hidden in history. Wagner's dramatic content as well as his scenery are *pictures* in a higher sense, real Imaginations—the technical term in anthroposophy for the image seen with inner vision, when this picture expresses a spiritual reality.

Already the sea and the sea-storm in *The Flying Dutchman* are such Imaginations, and the scenery in *Tannhäuser* even more so. The 'Venusberg' is the Imaginative picture for the whole sensually erotic 'complex' in the human make-up. The other two scenes in Acts I and III are also extremely pictorial. In the first place there is the spring landscape surrounding the Wartburg, rising up after the sinking of the Venusberg—how effective here are the shepherd's song and the bells of the flock after the sultry Venusberg music, which for the first time shows Wagner's complete gift of mastery in musical expression. And then in Act II, the same landscape in the garment of late autumn, with the falling leaves, with all the dying in nature. Here the contrast between blooming and withering stands effectively before our souls.

In contrast to these natural images, the scenery of Act II with the interior of the Wartburg directs us to historical acts, to that important period of Frederick II the Hohenstaufen (1212–1250), in which the life of St Elizabeth also falls. Rudolf Steiner pointed out what this epoch meant for the evolution of consciousness in humanity, how it was just round about 1250 that the earlier clairvoyance, excepting a few remnants, was in process of disappearing. For the understanding of Wagner's *Tannhäuser* this is an important consideration.

What the legend relates, Steiner, from spiritual research, makes more accessible. The legend tells how in a certain way the 'Mystery of the Star of Bethlehem' shines and works into the life of St Elizabeth already at her birth. Healing powers, which showed themselves in the child Jesus of Luke's Gospel, were also revealed in a similar manner in Elizabeth's childhood. Healing powers of love, like those of her contemporary, Francis of Assisi, were revealed in Elizabeth's maidenly being, in that purity which still remained spiritually hers, even when from the physical aspect she had become a wife and a mother. This is why Wagner, apparently defying history, gave her the virginal role. This has to be taken as a picture in the spiritual sense, not as outer history.

The same applies to Elizabeth's death by sacrificial love. In reality the expiration of her life was such a sacrifice of herself, even though outwardly different from that shown in Act I of *Tannhäuser*. Elizabeth carried within herself, in her childlike nature, in her chaste being and its healing powers, a part of the germinating Paradisal life; she carried something of the 'powers of the Tree of Life', we might say, using a biblical image. In possession of those forces, she saw herself placed into an epoch of humankind's descent, of the decay of the old forces in humankind; the decay of the Catholic Church, too, which later she met in its darkness in the problematical figure of Conrad von Marburg, to whom she sacrificed her purest forces with living patience. We may compare with this the way in which Wagner in *Tannhäuser* describes the character of the Pope who condemns the repentant sinner to hell. That is what the Church had become. The once budding stem of church-life was drying up, like the barren staff—one is reminded of a Bishop's crozier.

Into this withering life Elizabeth sacrifices the growing vitality of her virginal power, redeeming thus a part of ecclesiasticism. She helps all that still existed of the old powers that were, however, upon the path of decay; she gives it new life with the power of her pure love. This was likewise the case with Heinrich von Ofterdingen; this hero, romantically conjured by Novalis, in Wagner's work becomes Tannhäuser. The staff which grows green again in Act III is the pictorial expression, 'Elizabeth's prayer' the poetical and musical expression, of this sacrifice of transformation that lies completely within the Christian sphere. The woodwind instrumentation of this prayer, with its purity and deep inwardness, speaks of those powers of budding life. It is a meditative crossing of 'the threshold of the spiritual world' borne by one of the purest sacrificial moods.

This is also expressed in the music, for the 'key of balance, of the Scales',[21] Gb-major, as the transition from the higher, lighter keys (with sharps) to the lower, dark keys (with flats) represents, as elsewhere in Wagner, the 'crossing of the threshold' from the sensory world to the spiritual world, found in Titurel's consecration-experience in *Parsifal*, in the quintet in *The Mastersingers*, and other places. The combining of this perspective of the 'starry circle' with that of the planets[22] leads in this key to Venus, 'ruler in the Scales', Venus-Urania, that is, the heavenly Love that guides the soul through the portal of death, over the 'threshold of the spiritual world' back from the earthly to the heavenly homeland. This may be said here, because Wagner-Wolfram himself speaks of this in Act III of *Tannhäuser*:

> Like a presentiment of death, twilight covers the land, veiling the valley with a dark garment; the soul, longing for those heights, trembles after the flight through night and terror. But there shinest thou, loveliest of stars; thou sendest thy soft light afar, the mighty twilight is divided by thy kindly beam, and thy friendly ray shows the path out of the valley.

The 'loveliest of stars', in Wagner-Wolfram's mind, is the planet Venus and at the same time Elizabeth herself, who incorporates the true Venus, Love in the Christian sense. In her self-sacrificing death, she is finally revealed as Heavenly Love, and becomes for Tannhäuser, Venus-Urania.

Elizabeth is also the other aspect of Venus—'the healing power of Love'. Here the corresponding key—this can be demonstrated exactly—would be G-major. And Wagner indeed causes Elizabeth to appear at the beginning of Act II singing in this key ('You, dear hall'). In Act III, but already at the end of Act II, this chaste delight of love has given way to the earnest gravity of self-sacrificing love. In its very essence Wagner's music for Elizabeth reveals both sides of the being of Venus-(Love). She is the true Venus, filled with Christ.

It can be a splendid experience to realize the way in which Wagner develops all this step by step before us. Firstly, Venus of the Venusberg, the Venus who has become false and heathen, drawn down into human sensual nature. Then, Elizabeth as the true Venus full of Christ, at first pure as a child, hopeful as a child, healing and chaste; then as the solemn Venus of the sacrifice by death and the crossing of the threshold, the heavenly consoler and advocate. All this, right into the musical key, eloquent and right. And then, when all this has passed before us, Wagner makes Venus, the evening star, appear gleaming in the heavens. These are things which will be more clearly recognized some time in the future. A new star-wisdom, a Christianized astrology of the future, will recognize especially what Wagner's *Tannhäuser* signifies in this direction. Only then will a truly perceptive understanding of Wagner exist, one raised above sympathy and antipathy.

The concept of redeeming love, which in the last analysis is a thoroughly Christian thought, runs as a fundamental motive, in fact as the main motive, through all Wagner's creations. It is present already in *Die Feen*. Excepting the two music dramas of the Grail, this motive is linked everywhere with female characters—in the case of the Grail Knight this female element is completely assimilated into his own being. In the later works, the highpoints here are Isolde and Brünnhilde. Already in *The Flying Dutchman*, Senta incorporates this Christian *motive of redeeming love*. With this we have already come a step nearer to the Christian element in *The Flying Dutchman*.

From this point, let us look once more at *Tannhäuser*, especially at the historical scene in Act II. We have already spoken of the decay of the old powers of clairvoyance, also the decay of ecclesiastical

Christianity at that time. Why, after all, is Tannhäuser so heartlessly condemned in the 'singers' contest' scene on account of his Venus-berg-experiences? Are his judges better than Tannhäuser?

At this point we have to remember what has already been said about the disappearance of the old powers of clairvoyance at that time. When Tannhäuser undergoes his Venusberg-experience, rem-nants of that disappearing 'old clairvoyance' still remained. *Now* this vision has become degenerate, it has become entangled in the impure forces of the blood, in all that lives and weaves and undulates in the hidden depths of physical human nature. Rudolf Steiner frequently emphasized that just out of these physical depths frequently the most magnificent multicoloured, ensnaring 'astral visions' can arise. But a certain power of clairvoyance is still required. Apart from Tannhäuser, only Wolfram von Eschenbach among his contemporaries still pos-sessed this clairvoyance, in a purer way than Tannhäuser because he was more highly evolved. That is why in Act III, after Tannhäuser's outbreak of despair when he is condemned to hell by the Pope, the Venusberg arises once more before his spiritual eye—the whole thing is psychologically so obvious—also for Wolfram who is sympathet-ically related to him. In this remnant of clairvoyance, Tannhäuser differs from the others. Had they still possessed similar powers they would not have beheld better things, but only less beautiful, less mag-nificently colourful images. Neither are they better than Tannhäuser, they are only less gifted, their powers of soul, their powers of love, are weaker. But they do what religious hypocrisy and the sanctimo-nious have always done. From their moral high ground they condemn the 'fallen sinner', who has only had the courage to speak out frankly what the others shyly hide.

A radiant contrast to this world of decay is the virginal character of Elizabeth. In her lives the enduring, tolerating, forgiving, consoling, and self-sacrificing true Christian love. Through the sacrificial power of this love, she performs the miracle of transformation—the sterile wood of the staff which the Pope had cursed grows green again, full of germinating life. Out of the withered Christianity of the past a new, vitally powerful Christianity arises, radiantly blessing, bearing the future. If we think at the same time of the legend of St Elizabeth and the miracle of the roses, and if we connect the one picture—the sprout-ing rod—with the other, then the Mystery of the Rosy Cross arises. The time of Elizabeth, the beginning of the thirteenth century, is also the time when Rosicrucianism of the Middle Ages began. In his poetic fragment *'Die Geheimnisse'*, Goethe elucidated the Mystery of the cross surrounded by roses. The refining and transformation of forces evident in the human blood is the essential meaning of this symbol. This leads us once again to the Mystery of the Blood of Golgotha, to the 'Mystery of the Holy Grail'. Already in *Tannhäuser* in the budding rod, Wagner brings the 'miracle of Christian transformation', to which he gives the most perfect expression in the *Karfreitagszauber* in *Parsifal*. *Tannhäuser* gently touches on the 'Christianity of the Holy Grail'.

This reappears straightway in the next creation, *Lohengrin*, which is musically a stage riper and more self-possessed. We do not yet enter, as in *Parsifal*, the territory of the Grail itself. That territory still remains the 'land afar not approachable by your steps'. For this reason the motif seems all the more effective. The simple Grail-motif in *Lohengrin*, in bright, high A-major in which the first Prelude and again the Grail narration are introduced, sounds even more mysterious, more basically magical than all the Grail-motifs in *Parsifal*.

Like *Tannhäuser*, *Lohengrin* also leads us into that period of the Middle Ages when degenerate remnants of the old heathen consciousness still opposed the already decadent Christianity of the Church. In Ortrud and Telramund such powers from previous ties were still active, the ancient world of the Teutonic gods still survives, but everything is troubled, tending towards darkness, evil, and black magic. Ortrud's invocation of the old gods Wotan and Freya shrills frightfully through the night. The dark powers of black magic with all their horrors oppose the white, helpful magic of the Grail. Here, too, all-pious ecclesiasticism is no longer able to distinguish black from white, to recognize the lucid, transparent being of the Grail-initiate. Rudolf Steiner once spoke of the task of the 'initiate Lohengrin' in the Middle Ages.

Here again, we find ourselves in the sphere of 'Mystery occurrence' working behind the scenes of external worldly events. The essential thing in Wagner is the attitude that humankind takes towards the initiate, once he has come amongst them. Humankind gasps at him, but does not understand him. The ecstatic veneration, too, of the maiden rescued through the help of the Grail, is not yet pure, not yet free from that which works unperceived in the hidden depths of human nature. And thus Elsa too fails in the trial, without which you cannot enter the 'sphere of the initiate'. She puts the forbidden question; catastrophe breaks in. The initiate must sorrowfully withdraw from foolish humankind that will to help—which he manifests to the utmost and must return to the solitary sublimity of his Grail-world. Of all Wagner's dramas, the ending of *Lohengrin* is the most tragic. In his letters to Mathilde Wesendonck, Wagner himself calls it 'the most tragic of all poems, because reconciliation can only be found when one casts the widest possible view over the world', namely, the view of repeated earth-lives.

In contrast to *Parsifal*, which bears more significance for the future, *Lohengrin* is eminently a drama of the present-day. Today, too, the helping initiate, the teacher with knowledge, comes to humankind to awaken recognition of the 'secrets of Christianity'. But all the powers of darkness accuse him of heresy, and the others as well, those who do recognize him, only in isolated cases reach real understanding. Emil Bock[23] has drawn attention to the difference between the 'Elsa-question' and the 'Parsifal-question'. The Elsa-question is a question of intellectual curiosity. It is not this, however, but the heart-felt question, the Parsifal-question, which alone should be put to the initiate. With regard to higher knowledge most people today still put the question of curious Elsa. They still avoid the question of the heart.

In point of time, *Lohengrin* stands exactly in the middle between the creative work of the first half of Wagner's life and that of the second half, in which he finds his real style, the style of the music drama. We are not concerned here with these transitions from one style to the other, but the development of the Christian element in the sequence of single works. The Teutonic mythological world appears first in Wagner's work in *Lohengrin*, then, in the dimness of the later age of decaying consciousness, it completely governs *The Ring of the Nibelung*, the first great music drama. Viewed externally, the Christian element, as in *Tristan and Isolde*, recedes entirely. But we have already emphasized how the 'world-wide Christianity' of Wagner develops out of the background of the pre-Christian Mysteries. This is significant in *The Ring*, and above all in *Tristan and Isolde*.

Also in *Twilight of the Gods* in the *Ring*-cycle, the decay of the old consciousness of the gods is movingly revealed. The 'luciferic temptation' (Loki, or Loge), that in *The Rhinegold* approached first the gods and then later humankind, with the entrance of the powers of death, releases the 'ahrimanic power' (Alberich-Hagen). But already at the end of *The Rhinegold* there flashes up in Wotan the thought of the future, the thought of the ego, the 'I' (Sword-Motif in C-major), the thought of freedom, which later becomes the Christ-Impulse, the Christ Ego-Impulse of the future. Brünnhilde, the Valkyrie, the child of love—conceived through the ancient sibyl, the 'Vala'—takes up Wotan's thought. Sigmund, the first bearer of the sword of the gods—a sword not forged by himself, by the ego-concept—had failed and had had to be tragically sacrificed by Wotan himself to the opposing power. Then Brünnhilde, with helping love, braving in love her father's command, prepares the 'son', bearer of the future. Her love, fruitful for the future, conquers her father's wrath. This really deeply Christian scene in Act III of *The Valkyrie* is the most marvellous representation of the supreme power of love. Brünnhilde, the Valkyrie, is put to sleep by Wotan. The wall of waving flame, which can be penetrated and crossed only by the fearless initiate, separates her from the world of lower consciousness. Like Isolde, Brünnhilde is a bearer of the higher life-element. The Christian impulse of the future lives in her self-sacrificing love.

Emil Bock speaks impressively about this Mystery.

> Brünnhilde, surrounded by the wall of fire, is put into a deep sleep. She is that divine part which alone can survive. Will the human being one day arise from the depths of the Ring and gain the rock summit and, in spite of possessing the Ring, be strong enough to cross the trial zone of the fire of desire? Then he may be united with the last daughter of the gods—with the Eternal Feminine.

The 'Son' grows in the person of Siegfried, the fearless initiate and bearer of the ego-impulse—of the sword forged by himself—who conquers the dragon of the old coerciveness, breaking the spear of the old coercive legality wielded by Wotan himself, who opposed him on his way to Brünnhilde. But in him too, in his initiation—of which the music drama *Siegfried* is its pictorial representation—his 'ego-impulse', there remains a weak point. He draws down into a human relationship, that union with Brünnhilde which he should have left in the divine sphere, and Brünnhilde is sacrificed. Just as Tristan betrays Isolde, the higher life, destined for him by decree immemorial, to Marke, bearer of the old life, so Siegfried betrays Brünnhilde to lower human life, to the world of Gunter, Guntrune and Hagen. Hagen's spear strikes him on the spot where Brünnhilde's magic did not reach, on his backbone. It is the same spot where Christ bore the cross. In the Mystery of Golgotha, in Christian initiation, that which remained unfulfilled in the Siegfried-initiation is fulfilled. Parsifal is the perfected Siegfried. This is the direct connection of the Mystery of *The Ring of the Nibelung* with the Christian Mystery of *Parsifal*.

Similarly, *Tristan and Isolde*, Wagner's ever-living creation, which with its overflowing richness cannot be exhausted here, stands near to the Christian sphere. Here again, the pre-Christian initiation remains tragically unfulfilled. Here again the 'wound' appears with the same meaning. The dying Tristan sinks into the arms of Isolde, whom living he had not been able to win and not been able to retain. It is the same Mystery-motif as in Goethe's fairy tale of 'The Green Snake and the Beautiful Lily'—the Lily, like Isolde and Brünnhilde, is the 'higher life'. As stated by Wagner himself in his letters to Mathilde Wesendonck, the sick Tristan of Act III is the preliminary stage of the wounded Amfortas in *Parsifal*. Like Amfortas' wound, his wound is the wound of humankind as well, the wound of humanity's deep longing, which is healed only by Christ. *Tristan and Isolde* is the drama of humankind's great longing, which awakens the forces within us that lead to Christ, to the true blueprint of humanity.

Through this we also understand the various Christ-motives which in *Tristan* still seem united with that which appears pre-Christian, and we understand the riddle of the gospel language which at some points enters into Wagner's *Tristan*. So we find right at the beginning of Act I, the 'might to command over sea and storm'. He speaks of the 'might of the Mother' in such a way that we feel it is the magic might which in pre-Christian times was still actually bound up with the 'forces of the Mother', with the female life-element, until Christ includes them in the Ego. Christ stills the storm on the lake—which is a picture of much that is human—out of the power of the Ego: 'I AM, fear not.' At the beginning of his signs when he performs the miracle at Cana, He still turns to the force of the Mother. The 'walking on the water' related to the 'appeasing of the storm' is also paralleled in Act III of *Tristan and Isolde*, in Tristan's vision of Isolde walking over flowery blue waves. But what there remains in the sphere of longing and of dream finds in Christ its fulfilment in the awake 'I'. It is just the Christian Gospel that shows us how much 'wind and waves' signify in Tristan's world, too, right into the music of *Tristan and Isolde*, and in the same way we meet with these two motives indeed already in *The Flying Dutchman*— another step, too, towards the Christian understanding of the *Dutchman*. We also meet sacramental motives in *Tristan and Isolde*. In the 'draught of reconciliation' we often find the motive of the communion chalice sounding. In Tristan's vision, he says to Isolde, 'She brings me the last draught of comfort', which reminds us of the Holy Supper and the Last Rites. Isolde's final suffering, when in Act III she bends over

Tristan's corpse—musically this is the epitome of suffering—reminds us of the Christian Pietà image—the Mother bent over the dead body of the Son, or as it appears in the Parsival legend of the Middle Ages, Sigune with the corpse of her dead lover. Here too Wagner uses sayings of the Gospels: 'Do you remain dumb? One hour only, just for one hour wake for me!' We recall Christ's words addressed to Peter and the other disciples sleeping with him in Gethsemane, 'Could you not watch with me one hour?'

Let us in passing glance at *The Mastersingers* which, with *Tristan and Isolde* is Wagner's outstanding artistic achievement. Bock draws attention to the relationship existing between *Tristan and Isolde* and *The Mastersingers*. In Hans Sach's gentle determination, in his striving to unite Eva to young Stolzing, he justly sees a Christian, a Johannine motif. Significantly, everything takes place during St John's-Tide.

> Hans Sachs has his name-day on St John the Baptist's day (Midsummer Day). He himself is like John the Baptist, who prepares the way for One greater, who as a messenger of the Father walks before the Son: 'He must increase, but I must decrease.' The message of the Baptist: 'Change your thinking, the kingdom of heaven is at hand!' is announced by Hans Sachs with the song: 'Wake up, day is approaching!' Hans Sachs is the 'friend of the bridegroom' [John 3:29].

Bock vividly shows how this 'wake up', already prominent in the orchestral Prelude to Act III is also musically the counterpart and reverse of that yearning melody which in the introduction of Act III of *Tristan and Isolde* 'sounds into the releasing womb of night, so infinitely sorrowful'.

It is an experience of humankind—and in this, especially, lies the Christian significance of *The Mastersingers*—that is expressed in the 'Wake up!' chorus of Act III. The overall human element is never missing in Wagner's works. *Rienzi* already contains signs of it, also *Tannhäuser*, and still more *Lohengrin*. Then in *The Ring* we enter another sphere, a sphere of gods and mythology. In *Tristan and Isolde* more than elsewhere this overall human element recedes—the human being stands alone before the cosmos, the sea, the eternal stars. The solitude becomes all the more painful in the sorrowful and yearning Act III.

However, just this solitude in face of the cosmos was necessary for Wagner, that he might find his way through to the all-embracing human experience of *The Mastersingers*. This work, as no other by Wagner, allows us to stand 'firmly on the earth'. Not for nothing does the 'shoemaker' play in it such a role. This is the great and overwhelming fact, that one and the same mind could create both these works, which in their whole moods are so immensely different and yet related to one another by a mysterious inner link. Indeed, that it is just *Tristan and Isolde*, the greatest and most decisive experience in Wagner's life, which could release the all-embracing humanity of *The Mastersingers*. This lovable gift to humanity knows how to evoke music that can weave about the greyness of everyday life, and even around all the follies of humankind, all 'delusion', the charm of a music drawn from all the scents of the earth, even from the lilac-perfumed Midsummer Night itself. More even than in all the other works does the Christian element in Wagner reveal itself *in this*. The wing beats of the future, of the Christian future, of the Christian future of humanity, are heard sounding through *The Mastersingers*.

This masterwork, deeply related to *Tristan and Isolde* as *Tristan and Isolde* is to *Twilight of the Gods*—which, meanwhile, still had to be completed—forms a decisive preliminary stage towards Wagner's final work *Parsifal*, in which he has built the consecrated temple for the Christian Mystery that permeated his whole life. Here we do not wish to enter into the details of this work entirely dedicated to the 'secrets of Christianity', to the Mystery of the Holy Grail. In the author's book *The Parsifal Christ-Experience* particular aspects are elaborated.

The most significant feature of Wagner's *Parsifal* is that it shows how, in the period which knew Christianity only as a church confession of belief, the Christian *path of knowledge* was put before humankind as the 'pathway to the Holy Grail' with its many trials. Rudolf Steiner's anthroposophy is a method, the evolving of this pathway of thinking perception, corresponding to the consciousness of our age. In Wagner, in the Prelude to Act III of *Parsifal*, the pathway grows to a deep musical experience, to a kind of symphonic poem. The whole style of the music of Act III shows some new and singular characteristics pointing to the future, whereas other things in the music of *Parsifal* still contain the past. The new element, which in the influence of the Christ-Impulse will one day come in music too, is still fragmentary in *Parsifal*, is still in its beginnings.

It has already been pointed out that in *Parsifal*, the mysteries of the Blood of Golgotha shine right into the music. The Mystery of transformation, of transubstantiation, is perfected in the *Karfreitagszauber*, where in the gentle morning light of the first spring days, out of all the flower chalices the miracle of the earth, transformed and transfigured through Christ's sacrificial death, beholds us.

In *Parsifal*, especially as we look at Amfortas, at Kundry, and at Parsifal himself, we are overwhelmed by the gravity of the experience of Christ. With its many trials this experience stirs the inmost depths of the soul, and there in the depths and in the subconscious depths the struggle occurs. In the book, *The Parsifal Christ-Experience*, the present writer has attempted to show, in connection with scenes from Wagner's *Parsifal*-poem, how this experience meets the soul in the form of successive stages in the awakening of consciousness.

*

'Merlin'

O Merlin in your crystal cave
Deep in the diamond of the day,
Will there ever be a singer
Whose music will smooth away
The furrow drawn by Adam's finger
Across the meadow and the wave?
Or a runner who'll outrun
Man's long shadow driving on,
Break through the gate of memory
And hang the apple on the tree?
Will your magic ever show
The sleeping bride shut in her bower,
The day wreathed in its mound of snow
And Time locked in his tower?

Edwin Muir (1887–1959)

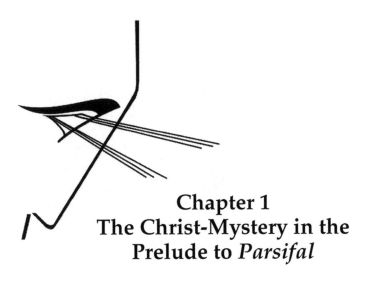

Chapter 1
The Christ-Mystery in the
Prelude to *Parsifal*

With the first notes of the Prelude, with the *Last Supper Theme*, the music of *Parsifal* places us at once into the heart of the Christ-world which governs the whole Mystery drama.[24]

Fig. 3

These notes of the Grail celebration sounding in Act I as the 'voices from the heights' from the uppermost dome of the Grail Temple, embracing the words of the Last Supper, 'Take this my body, take this my Blood, in token of our love', these same notes appear here in unison at the beginning of the Prelude, borne only by the strings and wind without any harmonic accompaniment, appearing *almost as the spoken word, as the words of love spoken by Christ from cosmic heights*. This 'Last Supper Theme' expresses not only something ritualistic or symbolic, but also the sublime experience of the cosmic chalice itself, the *Grail-experience* which addresses the innermost core of human consciousness, the 'consciousness-soul':[25] divine love which is sacrificed into Earth-existence is comprehended through love in the life of human beings.

As a poetic work, 'Parsifal' had been completed in 1877, and it appeared as a music drama in 1882 as the finale to Wagner's life's work. This is almost the date (1879) that the historical research of spiritual science sees as the threshold of the Michaelic Age. This age represents a step in the development of the consciousness-soul, which is summoned to raise the unfolding soul to the spiritual once again, after the passage of humankind through the zero-point of materialism. This realization of the consciousness-soul is something to which Rudolf Steiner drew attention in his philosophical works that appeals to human creative thinking that has found fruitful expression in many realms of practical life. It is the same experience of the consciousness-soul which—forty years after the appearance of *Parsifal*—is placed pictorially in the rite of The Christian Community, addressing people's religious sensibility. This is also called up at the very beginning of the Michaelic Age in Wagner's musical creation. The thought of the *Christ-Impulse* in the anthroposophical sense is something still difficult to grasp today. Only slowly does it reach the consciousness of the wider community. The material and technical progress of our day makes it difficult to grasp; the destiny of the Anthroposophical Movement shows this clearly enough.

Yet, in the artistic creation presented in Bayreuth it was given to humankind in musical form, and both before and after the turn of the nineteenth to the twentieth century many souls were strongly seized by it because in this work the *innermost depths of the human soul were somehow touched*. Something that comes through this musical work as a obscure feeling and which at first can easily remain in the unconscious depths of the soul can be seen today in *the age of the consciousness-soul* as something which should be brought into the full light of day. Today we need to appreciate Wagner's creation in order to reveal to the consciousness-soul, also known as the spiritual soul, to the 'I', the profound depths of knowledge that live magically both in Wagner's music as a whole and in the music and poetry of *Parsifal* in particular.

***

The theme at the opening of the Prelude, though often difficult to access for the 'musical expert', can be quite easily understood when it is accepted as something which speaks directly to the heart, as do all the themes of *Parsifal*. What matters is the soul's ability to rest upon the keynote, on each single note and interval, and to perceive inwardly what lies *between the notes*. Then the notes and intervals of the Last

Supper Theme, the full unfolding of this theme from keynote over third and fifth towards the world of sixth and seventh will reveal a whole new world.[26] The music of *Parsifal* should not be approached as a much-loved piece of music, but as a spiritual experience, *as a meditative experience*. It is only to the capacities of inner devotion and meditative surrender which are present germinally in almost every soul that the secrets of this music will be disclosed.

This theme of the Prelude is like a thought or a word meditated and worked upon in such a way that everything is inwardly quickened and acquires its own self-sustaining life. In the same way, the notes of this Last Supper Theme, this representation in music of Christ's words of love, are played at first in unison without any harmonic accompaniment, and are then woven about with an enlivening harmony. The key of A♭-major which dominates the Last Supper Theme, the key of secret-laden twilit darkness, corresponds both in the cycle of the year to the deepest dark, and to the experience in soul and spirit which leads down to the most profound depths of soul.[27] At the beginning the melody on its own (without harmony) is set against the harmony on its own (without melody), which then soon includes the notes of this theme.

When we understand how the *circle of fifths, of the twelve key-centres*, has an upper and a lower, a light and a darkness half (keys with sharps and keys with flats, respectively), we also appreciate A♭-major as the key of deepest mystical darkness, as the 'light in the darkness'. The darkness where light is absent would be the relative, F-minor. The key of A♭-major Wagner used appropriately for the *Liebesnacht*, the 'night of love' in *Tristan and Isolde*, and in *Parsifal* for the Grail experience. We can also appreciate why in *Lohengrin* the mysterious theme of the Grail in the Prelude, gleaming far off in the heights, and of the 'Grail narration', is heard in radiant A-major. The world of the Grail and the Grail-experience of *Parsifal*, in leading down into secrets of the blood profoundly met in meditation, are in tune with the dark night of A♭-major. The language of tonality is nowhere clearer than in Wagner's *Parsifal*.

We should hear this music of A♭-major at the beginning of the Prelude to *Parsifal* from a large Wagner orchestra, if possible in the acoustics of the Festival Theatre at Bayreuth, in order to recognize what Wagner did. Out of the simplest of all means and with instrumentation that had already existed for a long time, out of profound meditation, Wagner has conjured up a completely new experience in sound, something which again can only be fully comprehended in spiritual meditation.

***

For the meditative way of contemplation applied here, it will become apparent that the Last Supper Theme is divided further on into more simple motifs which later are used as such. A first independent motif lies in the first five notes of this theme, rising up to the sixth degree (the note F). Without thinking of special mystical contexts within the musical elements in terms of the 'meaning of the notes', but simply in looking at how Wagner himself uses these notes in the music of *Parsifal*, especially at the end of Act III, we could speak of the motif of *Christ's self-sacrificing love*.

Still more characteristic is the second motif of six notes, following the first motif within the Last Supper Theme.[28]

Fig. 4

An archetypal motif, a primal motif of suffering from the whole of Wagner's music stands before us in these six notes, which we can also find in the other music dramas, even in the opera *Tannhäuser*. Think above all of the shrill, flickering theme at the beginning of Act II of *Tristan and Isolde*, the 'Day Theme' full of suffering. In *Tristan and Isolde*, the day-world, the glaring torch of earthly day-consciousness, brings deception and suffering, whereas the realm of night, the cosmic night, is filled with truth and redemption in love.

Fig. 5

But when we compare with this the completely different expression, the peaceful gentleness and quiet resignation of the melodic sequence in the quite similar motif in *Parsifal*,

Fig. 6

then we will feel and recognize how very much this general 'suffering motif' of Wagner has become here the direct *expression of Christ's Passion*. As the self-sacrifice of *Christ's Love* appears in the first five notes of the Last Supper Theme, the motif of *Christ's Passion* appears in the subsequent six notes. Of all Wagner's themes, none has such power to become a meditative experience as this short 'Christ's Passion Motif'. The Last Supper Theme is the central theme of the *Parsifal* music, and this suffering motif is the centre of the Last Supper Theme itself. The more we follow this short motif throughout the whole music of *Parsifal* and the more we succeed to rest meditatively on the tranquil sufferings of these six notes, the more we shall find in it the innermost core of the music of *Parsifal* and its Christ-Mystery. Wagner, this singular dramatic artist and at the same time musical interpreter of human conflict, has movingly expressed quite unadorned, that suffering which is no longer human but divine, *suffering of the Godhead for human beings*.

Following on the *Motif of Christ's Love* as the first part of the Last Supper Theme, comes the *Motif of Christ's Passion* which is itself succeeded by a third motif. This again is characterized by five notes; the first four—the fifth descends again—is nothing but a simple rising scale.

Fig. 7

The most significant things in the *Parsifal* music are woven of the simplest musical elements. Here simple notes and intervals, scales, basic harmony would wish to be felt as expressing fundamental cosmic relationships. Taken by themselves and out of context, these four or five notes may not at first perhaps say anything essential to us, they may be felt only as 'a scale', or part of one. But if we observe how, through the whole work, this motif separates from the Last Supper Theme and is used independently in the most different places as the *Spear Motif*, then we can recognize in these notes the actual *Motif of the 'I' of Christ*. In the world of Grail Imaginations into which Wagner's *Parsifal* leads us, the *Spear* appears as *symbol of the 'I', or ego*. The ego has been pulled down by the adversary of humankind into the lower personal sphere of the instincts, desires and passions, where the human being is ensnared in egotism, in the crisis of sin, in the grip of the powers of death, in the fate of Amfortas.

However, through Christ the 'I' is returned to the divine and becomes the redeeming power in which the human being finds true perfection. 'The wound can only be healed by the very same spear which caused it.' In succumbing to the temptation of the lower soul-region in Klingsor's magic garden, Amfortas, the sinful Guardian of the Grail, loses the Holy Spear, the unconquerable weapon of the 'I', the will within the 'I', to Klingsor, the enemy of the Grail. Amfortas receives, from his own spear hurled from Klingsor's hand, the wound which will never be healed, for which there is no cure. The wound is only healed when the innocently-pure Parsifal, led by Providence, is faced with the same temptation as Amfortas, and resists victoriously. In this way he wrests from the adversary the Holy Spear which cannot strike him, to return it to the Grail Castle, where it heals the wound which once it struck.

In the centre of the whole drama of *Parsifal* and of *the drama of humankind* stands this *Spear Motif of the 'I', or ego*, which, having become serviceable to the tempter as 'lower ego', strikes the wound of humanity, which is then healed by the Higher Ego, the Christ Ego. In Wagner's music it is always denoted by those five notes—four actual notes of the rising scale—notes which again are a constituent of the Last Super Theme. Not yet within this theme itself but wherever the Spear Motif as such is used independently, these four notes emerge with a particular *marcato*—notated by Wagner himself in the score—rising in a simple, direct, diatonic, and sharply-contoured way. The Holy Spear is an image of the 'I' united with the divine, with Christ as the victorious, insurmountable power, safely and surely passing between the adversaries to left and right. In the whole formation of the notes, this theme makes us recall the word, 'but passing through the midst of them he went away' (Luke 4:30).

We hear the *Motif of Christ's Love* appearing in the first five notes of the Last Supper Theme, the *Motif of Christ's Passion* in the next six notes; and in the following four or five notes always related by Wagner to the 'Spear', the grand *Ego Motif* of Christ as the third part of the Last Supper Theme, of Him who can majestically hold His own against all adversaries, Who unswervingly leads the way through the midst. The Last Supper Theme of *Parsifal* in its three single motifs places before us the *loving, suffering, victorious* Christ. Looking at the last three notes which follow the third motif and with which the Last Supper Theme concludes we can no longer speak of a special 'motif', but nevertheless hear how together they express the restoration of inner equilibrium through Christ, of 'resting within the "I"' ('*Ruhe im Ich*').

Fig. 8

***

The Prelude to *Parsifal* is divided into certain large sections, deviating from Wagner's usual style. These sections close in the tonic and are even separated through pauses and fermata from what follows. This is something almost unheard of in Wagner's music-drama style, but which *Parsifal* furnishes very characteristic exceptions. The spiritual significance of this fact will become clearer below. The first development of the Last Supper Theme, fading away in syncopated A♭-chords, is now followed by another similar theme. Again we find here the simple thought fashioned like words, which is taken into the feeling realm by being surrounded with harmonic accompaniment, and is thus quickened as in meditation. (Musical thoughts are embodied in melody, an element of feeling is involved in harmony, and an element of will in rhythm.) This time everything seems to have moved into a still deeper darkness—the key of A♭-major appears to shift over to C-minor. Wagner, however, has left the key signature of A♭ on purpose—everything should still be felt as lying within the sphere of A♭-major.[29]

C-minor, the darkest depths of the circle of fifths, appears here within the inwardly shining world of A♭-major as the solemn dark of the innermost sanctuary where the mysteries of the Blood are now accomplished: 'Take this my Blood, take this my Body, in remembrance of me.' Thus run the words when the theme returns sung later on in the Grail celebration in Act I. The painful suspensions sound here in the harmonic development still more intimate, filled with still more suffering than in the initial A♭-major section. Yet the whole episode stands fully symmetrical with the first part purely in A♭-major. Both together create the actual first section of the Prelude. In dark C-minor, this first part dies away in dissolving, syncopated C-minor chords, Christ's words of Love spoken from cosmic heights.

***

Christ's words of Love spoken from cosmic heights—the twice-developed Last Supper Theme—is followed by something like an awakening call, still before the actual commencement of the second section. This call, a kind of transition theme, seems like a solemn admonition to hear this divine speech now with human ears, and is first played by trumpets and trombones, then gently carried into the heights by the woodwind.

Fig. 9

These are the same notes that sound later on right at the beginning of Act I as the 'Awakening Call' that rouses the sleepers. 'He, Ho! You guardians of the woods, or rather, guardians of sleep, at least wake up at morn!' followed by 'Do you hear the call? Give thanks to God that you are chosen to hear it!' During the at first mystic-quiet, then pithy, sonorous sounds of this motif, we see the Grail Castle appear in Act I.

And somehow in this basic, simple theme the picture of the rising castle is always connected with awakening into consciousness, with advancing inner awakening.

The prosaic character and sobering effect of this 'Awakening Call' corresponds at the same time to the condition of the consciousness-soul standing before its own emptiness until it finds its fulfilment from above, from the spirit—that which spiritually fills its emptiness. Faced with this fact, borrowing of certain sounds from Mendelssohn's 'Reformation' Symphony has no real significance. With other themes, also in *Parsifal*—think of the prophecy 'enlightened through compassion' with its eloquent chord sequence—Wagner has fully shown his creative power of invention.

The later dramatic use of this 'Awakening Call' theme sweeps away all reminiscence, especially where it takes on a visionary expression, shifting from the original primitive use of harmony into distant and strange keys, as in Act II with Parsifal's vision of the Grail. Again at the end of Act II, this theme achieves a magic effect, in this case, through a heightened diatonic simplicity in the key of C-major, reminiscent of the 'Spear Motif' with its ascending progression of parallel sixths, and it strikes the 'false splendour' of Klingsor's magic castle into ruins.

***

This 'Awakening Call', appearing as a mere transition motif, closes in the dominant, E♭-major. The actual second section of the Prelude follows, beginning again in the Grail key of A♭-major. It begins with the development of that simple, prominent motif which is usually called the '*Faith Motif*' because it embraces the words 'Faith lives, the dove hovers' in the well-known part of Act I. It expresses what *the human soul answers* to the divine Word of Love spoken from cosmic heights. In pure musical form, this motif

Fig. 10

is actually the inversion of another motif already heard within the Last Supper Theme as the 'Spear Motif', the Christ-Ego Motif. The scale which there ascends

Fig. 11

here descends.

Fig. 12

There a rising up into the cosmic, here a turning inwards, a taking in of the revelation of the Christ-Ego and Christ's Words of Love into the human 'I'. The Word spoken from cosmic heights resounding in the human soul, is answered here. In what can this response solely consist? Nothing less than the complete and ceaseless offering of the individual to the divine, expressed in The Act of Consecration of Man [the Eucharistic rite of The Christian Community], following the priest's communion of the bread. The content of this 'Faith Motif' cannot be 'faith' in the sense of a mere external, dogmatic belief. Even when the subject of 'faith' appears in the Gospels, or in Paul too, something else is meant, something anchored more deeply in the heart's foundations. It is not less but more than an intellectual knowledge of the understanding. Who has really understood John's 'all who believed in his name' (John 1:12)? It should be recognized that the Greek *pisteuein*, 'to believe', standing there throughout the original text, is actually an untranslatable word. This belief, or faith, is only then realized when knowledge is awakened within the heart and borne by heart-forces. *Pistis*, 'faith/ belief', is connected with 'firm', only that which has become inner firmness of the heart, resounds in the heart like a 'firm castle', has been built as a Grail Castle. Rudolf Steiner spoke on an occasion of importance for humankind about a 'foundation stone to be laid into the heart'—that is faith in the Johannine sense, which is also the 'sense of Parsifal', the 'sense of the Grail'. The 'I' of Christ speaks to humans in the 'Last Supper Theme', and humans immerse their certainty of heart in the Christ-'I' in the 'Faith Motif'. That is the true meaning of Christian 'faith'.

Luther felt this when he received inspiration for his hymn 'A stronghold sure is our God' ['A safe stronghold' in Carlyle's version], and actually something of its spirit, without its being taken as a model, lives in the brazen trumpet and brass sounds of the 'Faith Motif' and its majestic development in the Prelude. Whoever finds this thought concerning Wagner's *Parsifal* 'too protestant' might recall what Steiner meant by the 'foundation stone in the heart'. For basically, Luther's 'stronghold sure' is something similar. Hyper-modern people, for whom everything only vaguely reminiscent of this hymn is an annoyance, might consider how even Bruckner, and especially Bruckner, when striving after a culmination in his great symphonic works, finds it in several prominent cases in a hymn tune carried by the sonorous strength of brass instruments. In the last movement of his *Ninth Symphony*, this hymn of Bruckner appears as though transfigured, unearthly, in a more delicate instrumentation.

In *Parsifal*, too, this brazen admonishing sound of trumpets and trombones of the 'stronghold sure', or the 'foundation stone of the heart', is only one side of the 'Faith Motif'. 'Faith' (*pistis*) itself, as an experience touching the soul in its very foundations, shows another side that can be compared with the delicate unfurling of flower chalices. In anthroposophy we hear of the awakening of higher organs of perception, what are called 'lotus flowers', among which the 'lotus flower of the heart' stands in the centre. The Ancient Indians in yoga, from clairvoyant vision, also speak of the 'twelve-petalled lotus flower in the heart'. For them, the heart was still the *means of knowing, the only true human knowing*; they saw this knowledge in unawakened people but as covered, obscured by the layer of external sensory illusion and delusive intellectual knowledge of the understanding. In *Parsifal* this leads us quite closely again to the theme 'enlightened through compassion'.

We notice how Wagner's 'Faith Motif' in the Prelude, after a first section in E♭-minor—the key of the spiritual threshold[30]—sounds once again with the Awakening Call, this time with a more tender expression pointing to the 'inner awakening' and leads over to a delicate development of the 'Faith Motif' in the woodwind, later joined by the strings. Then the strong, brazen expression of the 'certainty of heart' changes place with that of the 'inner chalice experience'. We meet this tender expression of the Faith Motif again later, especially with the transition to the *Karfreitagszauber* in Act III. Here, Kundry receives baptism from Parsifal and lies weeping at his feet. The decisive change is accomplished within her—the 'lotus flower of her heart' begins to unfold.

The development of the 'Faith Motif' in *Parsifal*, in its marked simplicity and the elevated, majestic working-out of the contrasts through the incisive instrumentation, does not fail to impress the receptive and musically unsophisticated listener. The 'musician' might find some things too primitive here, might see in the discords the modern 'atonal' musical style, to which Wagner, by the way, especially in *Parsifal* (in the Klingsor music, Act II) from conscious experience comes justifiably quite close. The traditionally trained musician may miss the 'solid counterpoint' of Bach's polyphonic art in the melodic lines of Wagner's 'Faith Motif'.[31] But in the Prelude it all depends on this primitive, marked simplicity, or on this clarity of musical expression that is hammered into the soul. Nietzsche found the right word for it in an extremely noteworthy letter—to which we shall return—where he praises the 'epigrammatic distinctness of this music, one is reminded by it of a shield of exalted workmanship'. Christ's Words of Love were fully to resound in *everyone*, especially in the simplest and plainest souls, so that musical expression had to be completely simple, strong and universally human. In the future a Mystery art might evolve to express the Christ-experience in a totally different musical language, hardly to be imagined today, but at the beginning of the new age everything had to be presented as simply as possible.

***

This part of *Parsifal* also dies away in the Grail key of A♭-major. The third part, in the same key, begins while horns and a timpani-roll in deepest bass quietly sustain the tonic which has now been reached. What new element comes? Nothing new, in as much as it returns again to the familiar Last Supper Theme. Yet this time it does appear changed. Before the theme commences a dark undertone is given to it through the vibrating F of cellos and basses in the depths; a sombre element is added, pointing to F-minor. If A♭-major is the mystical 'light in the darkness', F-minor is deepest dark without light. We see Christ's Words of Love penetrate the dark depths of the earthly, human sphere. The divine Blood is sacrificed to the blood-darkness of the earthly, human realm. The wonder of the Incarnation, to which the whole sequence of notes and intervals contains an indication—if we follow Rudolf Steiner—seems to sing gently in this touching of heights and depths. In this touching, the divine Words of Love, the Blood of Christ sacrificed into the depths of the Earth begins to *shine*. Just after the commencement of the theme, where the second part appears, the Motif of Christ's Passion, a wonderful glimmering and glittering begins in the upper strings, taken over from the vibrating basses. The artistic means used, with all its simplicity and commonness (Bruckner, following Wagner, makes much use of string tremulos), seems to be something unheard of, never present before in Wagner, especially here in this eloquent clarity of expression. Through this development the Passion Motif especially is brought out of the Last Supper Theme by being led through expressive modulation, like the outcry of Christ's Passion sounding through the whole world.

A depth and solemnity unheard of sounds from this divine experience of suffering in this 'Passion Motif', lights up in this glimmering and glittering in the strings. This would conjure up in us something like starlight twinkling within streaming blood. All this sounds again in characteristic places in the music drama, especially in the Amfortas scene of Act I, before the actual Grail celebration, 'The divine content of the sacred vessel glows with radiant glory', where the 'fount of holy Blood' is spoken of, and again, immediately following, 'here through the wound like His, struck by a blow from that same spear'. Similarly with Parsifal's vision of the Grail in Act II, 'My dull gaze is fixed on the sacred vessel, the holy Blood glows'. These words only confirm what can be felt in the Prelude from the music alone without this verbal explanation. The experience of the Blood from Golgotha stands there before the listener's soul, when receptive not only musically but also in soul and spirit. This episode of the Prelude especially can be quickened to a shining Imagination.

Steiner once described how clairvoyant vision, beholding the Deed of Golgotha, can perceive how the Blood dripping from the wounds of the Crucified etherises, as it were, and begins to light up, raying out into cosmic expanses. And he often related that if a spiritual eye from without had been able to look down to the Earth when the drops of Blood dripped into the Earth, it would have seen how in that moment the Earth, which until then had been darkened, began to shine once more like a star. And he added that the processes as they happened then, perceptible only to clairvoyant vision, have in reality encompassed the whole substance of the Earth, and that they will continue to work in the Earth until it is restored to cosmic Sun-like, star-like life by radiating once more from within.

Such words from a spiritual investigator never should be received simply dogmatically. The soul can come to understand in different ways. A period of continued living with The Act of Consecration of Man, in the Mystery of the Last Supper—experienced in ritual—with patience and inner offering, can and will sooner or later open up an entry into such experiences. This entry can also be found completely inwardly, in pure, devout meditation, in *an inner experience of the Last Supper*. The guidance of destiny might also play a helpful role. The following case taken from life is not invented, for we speak here out of our own experience.

Whilst listening to the Prelude to *Parsifal*, which expressively paints the Blood-experience of Golgotha in music, the soul receives an impression touching deeply on inner cosmic secrets. This impression does not perhaps become a fully conscious one, yet remains—to start with—more in the sphere of the feelings. It appears for a long time as if erased and forgotten as it sinks into the subconscious. Then the same person meets much later, again led by destiny, a spiritual researcher like Rudolf Steiner—perhaps in outer life, perhaps only in the written word. He hears such a declaration about the secrets of Golgotha. If he had heard it unprepared, according to destiny, the sense of these words would have been obscure for him, perhaps for a long time 'hard' for him—as it is called in Dante's *Divine Comedy*. His thinking, used to the earthly-material concerns, faced with the range of such cosmic visions, would have proved weak.

Now, however, the words of the spiritual researcher touch on this long-forgotten, almost obliterated impression the soul had received at a certain time from this music. What was sunk into the depths of the subconscious all of a sudden penetrates with power and knocks at the gates of consciousness. The once dim impression has become a living conception. A true contact has been taking place with that world from which Wagner drew his musical inspiration, and from which the spiritual researcher spoke in clear, conscious spirit-vision. Let it be said once more: All this should not be taken dogmatically, but perhaps will give occasion for seeking a meditative understanding of this passage in the Prelude concerning us here, at the same time win access with this understanding to the words of the spiritual researcher.

In looking at the secrets of the Blood and secrets of the Earth touched on here, we shall understand better why the Last Super Theme—again, the self-enclosed Christ's Passion Motif—appears as *transformed* with its return in the third part of the Prelude, why it seems to speak here of the Mystery of *transformation* and *transfiguration*, or a new lighting up of the Earth into the activity of a star. It is as if a celestial star-life is communicated to the Earth, flashing out in the Blood from the wounds of the Crucified One, as if the Earth were to be illuminated and radiate before us in cosmic starlight. The Mystery of transformation, of *transubstantiation*, appears to be pushed into the foreground in the third section of the Prelude.

Placing all this before ourselves, let us pause a moment. We approached the Prelude as a meditative experience, perceiving how it is divided into simple themes and sections. So far, the yield of spiritual content of these sections for meditative contemplation—does it not remind us of something well-known, of the division and construction of the Mass, which has received a new formation in The Act of Consecration of Man of The Christian Community, a form in which new life has arisen corresponding to humankind's change of consciousness?

The whole structure of the Prelude to *Parsifal*: the divine Words of Love spoken from cosmic heights in the first section; the offering up of the human soul in the second section; the Mystery of transformation connected to the secrets of the Blood from Golgotha, the transubstantiation as a real earthly event in the third section—does it not present the separate parts and sections of the Mass and The Act of Consecration of Man: the Gospel, Offertory, Consecration (Transubstantiation)? Does the indication receive a new significance, the indication of the connection of Wagner's *Parsifal* with the impulses of the consciousness-soul, which in anthroposophy have found cognitive expression, and in the rite of The Christian Community religious expression?

When these kinds of questions are presented, we have to guard against the misunderstanding that Wagner somehow intended to base his Prelude on the scheme of the Mass—especially as The Act of Consecration of Man was given forty years later. Quite obviously that cannot be the case. True ritual forms are not arbitrarily thought out. They originate from the same profound depths which are also touched in meditative life. There the soul sees itself facing the great cosmic drama enacted between humankind and the divine from the very beginning. All this is also reflected in the single parts of the Mass, of The Act of Consecration of Man, which have emerged from the ancient Mysteries. The inner structure is present for meditative experience, even when a conscious modelling on certain forms in rituals handed down externally is not looked for. That structure has also found its way into the Prelude to *Parsifal*, and meets us there in a musical form. Thus far we have been able to find the first three parts of the Eucharist—Gospel, Offertory, Transformation, or something corresponding to them, in the Prelude.

But how about the *Communion*, the fourth part of the Mass, The Act of Consecration of Man. Does it, too, have its corresponding part in the Prelude to Wagner's *Parsifal*?

The most complete expression of the experience of Communion in *Parsifal* is the Grail celebration at the end of Act III, after the Grail Spear has been returned to the sanctuary and has healed the wound of Amfortas. Chalice and Lance, the two holy, archetypal symbols, are united once again, thus making the Grail celebration possible again. Like fructifying rain, life-giving dew quickening the thirsting earth, the long-missed cosmic mercy and miraculous grace of the Holy Grail, seen pictorially in the hovering descent of the white dove upon the assembled Grail Knights, alights at the end of Act III. It all finds its eloquent expression in a delicate figuration of the 'Faith Motif', like a graceful purling down from cosmic heights. The conclusion of *Tristan and Isolde* appears as a final apotheosis, an ecstatic streaming out into cosmic spaces; the conclusion of *Parsifal* is like a first tender streaming in from the cosmos, a first wellspring that in the future will increase and grow to an ever-wider and mightier stream. Compare John 4:13ff.: 'Every one who drinks of this [the earthly] water will thirst again, but whoever drinks of the water that I shall give him [that the 'I' gives him] will never thirst; that water that I shall give him will become in him a spring of water welling up to eternal life.'

That first part of the Last Supper Theme which we described as the sacrifice of Christ's love into the Earth appears, together with the 'Faith Motif', as the main motif of this experience of the Grail

Communion in Act III. This theme [the first part of the Last Supper Theme], delicately united with the 'Motif of the pure simpleton' which sounds now like the fulfilment of the prophecy ('made wise through compassion'), surrounds the decisive concluding words, 'Highest healing wonder! Our Redeemer redeemed!', where it is led characteristically through many keys, through the whole zodiac of keys.

We also find the same motif, however, as the 'Communion Motif' (the marriage of the divine with the human) at the conclusion, in the very last bars of the Prelude to *Parsifal*. Naturally here it does not yet appear in the far-flung, majestic development striding through the zodiac of keys as in Act III, but first as a quiet and distant sound, gently led upwards from octave to octave. We see the Prelude ending with a touch of Communion, which as such is fully manifested only at the end of the music drama.

Nietzsche's letter to his musical friend Peter Gast, mentioned above, telling of the deep impression he received from a performance of the Prelude to *Parsival* in Monte Carlo, ends with the words: 'Has any painter ever depicted such a sorrowful look of love as Wagner in the concluding strains of his Prelude?' There could not be a more apt characterization than these words for this 'touch of Communion' in the last fading bars of the Prelude, painful yet full of love, quietly hovering on the dominant seventh chord of A♭-major. And perhaps it allows the question about the painter who expresses similar things to be answered with a reference to Leonardo da Vinci. In the last bars of the Prelude there lives something of the sorrowful look of love as we see it in portraits of Christ and John the Baptist by Leonardo da Vinci. A gentle inner connection in general exists between Leonardo and Wagner's *Parsifal* music.

***

A few motifs still remain unmentioned in these observations on the Prelude. These lie between the actual 'Consecreation episode'—where in the third section of the Prelude the glimmering, glittering in the strings begins, pointing to the Mysteries of the Blood from Golgotha where the cry of Christ's Passion sounds through the world—and this sad, loving look within the last bars, indicating the 'Communion'. Essentially everything originates in *one* theme, with the 'Spear Motif of the Ego' which we recognize in the accents of the rising notes linking beginning and end.

Fig. 13

This motif first appears in Parsifal's vision of the Grail (Act II): 'My dull gaze is fixed on the sacred cup', with the words: 'Gentle, sacred bliss of redemption trembles through everyone's soul; but here in my heart the agony will not disappear, I hear the Saviour's cry surrounding the desecrated sanctuary.' It also appears where the 'Transubstantiation' leads over to this singular chromatic motif. We see that this motif of Wagner has to do with the Christ Mystery within the human soul, with the advancing and further working of transubstantiation within people, which give rise to the Mystery of the Grail. The actual Christ themes in *Parsifal*—so to speak, being on the side of the divine—are revealed in diatonic simplicity. Those themes pointing towards the soul-conflict in people are chromatic; something that is recognized in Wagner's musical style. We feel immediately this motif of soul-conflict. It is not so easy to memorize, it does not just pour into our heart like other motifs of the Prelude, but it stirs something within the heart. Further on, the motif appears once again in a somewhat changed form, with a characteristic turn indicating the 'experience of conscience'. It often returns in this form later on, yet it is essentially the same motif.

The names usually used, such as 'Agony-of-Sin Motif' and 'the Redeemer's Lamentation Motif', are not wrong, but they do not reach its core. Without wanting to analyse mystically the 'meaning of the notes', let us simply see how Wagner makes use of this important motif in the music drama—its importance in many ways has not yet been recognized. We find that it has to do everywhere with *eyes*, with

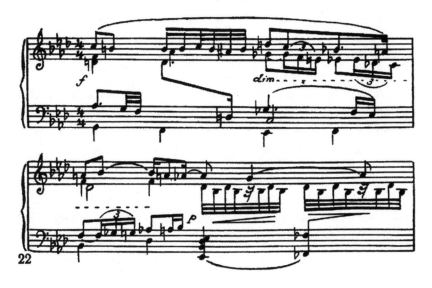

Fig. 14

the *gaze*. (Detailed evidence will be gone into in Chapter II; only a pre-liminary suggestion will be given here.) Expressed still more clearly, it appears that in this motif some sort of *process takes place between the eye and the heart*.[32] The look of Christ, the look from an eye full of divine love, meets the human soul. There the very love, the divine love from which man has become estranged since the Fall, the very light, the divine light within the 'I', lost or forgotten by man in sinful darkness, *that* stirs up a conflict within the human soul. The same kind of conflict in John's Gospel is always called *'crisis'* [AV/KJV, 'judgment']. That is easily misunderstood today if we lean too much on human notions and circumstances, for Christ does not 'judge' like a human judge. And yet this word in German (*richten*) is especially expressive as it contains the word *'ich'* ['I', ego]. In Christ the lost divine Ego of humankind has returned among men and this fact especially peo-ple are unable to endure; it makes them 'lift stones against him', as impressively described in John's Gospel. In its very way of leaving humanity free, causing the 'division of spirits' (crisis), lies the judging element of the divine Ego.

This theme in John's Gospel also dominates in the Christ-drama of Wagner's *Parsifal*. In the music, the above-mentioned 'Gaze Motif' always appears in some form. It always has to do with the gaze of Christ. That look which, through the love it radiates forth at the same time, wakes up the admonishment within the heart; the conflict in the soul leads to an inner split of consciousness. This seeming antithesis, the apparent contradiction of love and of reproach, punishing, sternly judging, comes to the fore in the effect resulting from that gaze of Christ as in a mysterious synthesis.

The Ego Motif of the Spear, which is mostly connected with the Gaze Motif, points to how in the deepest foundations this whole crisis in the heart will be set in motion through the divine Ego; it is a matter of wrestling for self-knowledge, for inner consciousness.

**

Before moving on in the next chapter to discuss the whole 'Christ-drama', let us return to that letter of Nietzsche, to a very remarkable passage, indeed as the most apposite of all characterizations of the Christ-experience meant here and the attendant soul-conflict. In the history of humankind, the very existence of this letter is a singular document for this experience of Christ, this Christ-conflict within the human soul.

After Nietzsche praises in the Prelude this 'clarity of music as descriptive art, which reminds one of a shield of masterly workman-ship'—this relates especially to the beginning, the 'Faith Motif', and so on—he still finds something else in his conclusion, prompting us to think of that chromatic motif and what underlies it, namely, 'a sub-lime and exceptional feeling, experience, event of the soul in the very essence of the music, which affords Wagner the greatest respect, a *syn-thesis of conditions* which many people, even "sophisticated people" hold to be mutually exclusive, of severity of judgement, of *"elevation" in the frightening sense of the word, of an accompanying knowledge and pen-etrating vision which cuts through the soul as with knives—and of a com-passion with what is beheld there and judged.'* And he adds, 'Only with Dante is there anything similar, nowhere else.' We can work our way through whole tomes of theology, old and new, and not meet such depth as in these salient sentences of Friedrich Nietzsche.

It is so exceptionally remarkable because we know that when Nietzsche wrote this letter (dated 21 January 1887) he had already arrived for a long time at the inner opposition which had found expression in the well-known writings against Wagner. The once pro-found, deeply-rooted relationship for which Nietzsche had found such sublime words in his aphorism 'star-friendship',[33] had already been turned into its opposite for a long while. Whence came this tragic revulsion? Mainly just because of *Parsifal*, which at least gave the last decisive offence. Nietzsche, the pastor's son, who perhaps just because of this was thoroughly disgusted with ecclesiastical Christianity, lived and talked himself over the years into an ever deeper hatred against everything Christian, a hatred which gripped his whole being, taking possession of his ego ever more completely. Nietzsche, the one-time deep admirer of *Tristan and Isolde* could not forgive his friend, Richard Wagner, who finally, in writing *Parsifal*, 'fell on his knees before the Christian cross'.[34] A ruling conflict between the two, present from the beginning with the question of Christ despite all subsidiary links, is completely revealed here. From now onwards the breakdown was decisive.

With this, we touch on the actual significance of this letter. Nietzsche, the declared opponent of Wagner, whilst under the impression of the Prelude heard for the first time, wrote such sentences of deepest admiration and at the same time highest objective understanding for Wagner's *Parsifal* music. More than this, he, feeling so hostile towards Christ, characterized on this occasion the inner core of the Christ-experience and the soul-conflict bound up with it, with a profound and at the same time so felicitous expression for which we would search in vain in whole volumes of theology. Do we not find revealed in all clarity the essence of the Christ-experience as meant here and the 'split of consciousness' connected with it? Is not this letter of Nietzsche itself the most striking of all documents for the Christ-conflict in the depths of the human soul? Do we not experience here in a singular way, how the *depths of consciousness* speak differently from how the surface consciousness thinks, or imagines to think?

Nietzsche attacks Wagner, the one-time friend, with whom he is still united above the temporal level in the innermost, rooted, star-depths of his being. And he blasphemes Christ, Who, however, is his—and each individual's—true Self in the depths of their being. Some sort of occasion prompted by destiny, as in this case the first hearing of the Prelude in Monte Carlo, tore open for a moment the whole befogged consciousness and from the mysterious depths of his true being the whole 'star-friendship' with Wagner spoke again, Christ spoke, the lost and blasphemed divine Ego.

The brief indication about Dante at the end of the letter points in the same direction. We know how Nietzsche otherwise spoke disparagingly about Dante, how once he called him 'the hyena who composes in graves'. Here, in the whole context with Christ, in the whole split of consciousness effected through the Christ-experience of this letter, Nietzsche places Dante as a measure for something most sublime. About Dante, too, the depths of consciousness in Nietzsche speak differently than does the surface.

As a conclusion to this first chapter dedicated to the Prelude, and at the same time as a preparation to the second on the dramatic element of the Christ-experience, we quote here that part of the previously partially-cited letter, especially its conclusion referring to the Prelude, as an historical illustration:

> Lastly—recently I heard for the first time the Prelude to *Parsifal* (namely in Monte Carlo!). When I see you again I will tell you exactly what I received there. Apart from the extra subsidiary question (for what *can or should* such music serve?) but put purely on the aesthetic level: has Wagner ever done anything *better*? The highest of all states of psychological awareness and certainty, the shortest and most direct form for what is said, expressed, *delivered*, each nuance of feeling led right up to the epigrammatic; a clarity of music as descriptive art, with which one thinks on a shield of masterly workmanship; and lastly, a sublime and extraordinary feeling, experience, event of the soul in the very essence of the music, which affords Wagner the greatest honour, a synthesis of conditions which many people, even 'sophisticated people', hold as impossible to combine, of severe judgement, from 'elevation' in the frightening sense of the words, from an accompanying knowledge and penetrating vision which cuts through the soul as with knives[35]—and of a compassion with what is beheld there and judged. Only with Dante is there anything similar, nowhere else. Has any painter ever depicted such a sorrowful look of love as Wagner in the final strains of his Prelude?
>
> Truly yours, Friedrich Nietzsche.

Chapter II
The Drama of the Christ-
Experience in *Parsifal*

If the Prelude to *Parsifal* allows us to experience the divine element of
the Christ-Mystery, the self-sacrifice of Christ's love, then the drama
of *Parsifal* depicts the changed human soul-experience. The self-sacrificing love of Christ stirs up dramatic conflict in the human soul;
Christ's loving gaze stirs up torment there. This dramatic conflict of
sin in the soul, this torment of the heart inwardly fought through, is
awakened in such a way that ultimately this same gaze of Christ can
rest upon man as a redeeming gaze. Already before the actual concluding bars of the Prelude, we heard the motif which in the music
of *Parsifal* is always connected with this soul-sin-crisis, with this torment of the heart. The term 'Gaze Motif', as we called it, we shall
retain in what follows.

The Christ-drama of *Parsifal* is built up in about seven episodes or
'scenes'. It will be shown how these scenes contain an experience of
developing consciousness, advancing from stage to stage. Consciousness increasingly lights up through the deepest soul-crises from stage
to stage, until the redemption in Christ, the deliverance in the self
is found. The Christ-Passion Motif in the music of *Parsifal*, linked in
many ways with the 'Gaze Motif', expresses in which way the divine,
Christ participates in human soul-conflicts and sin-conflicts, and to
what extent this is a concern of Christ. And it shows in as much as
the Spear Motif (Ego Motif) stands for the whole soul-crisis fought
through here, basically a crisis of the self, an ego-decision, a human
decision for the Divine 'I', or Ego, the Higher Self.

SCENE 1: *The Swan*

In Act I of *Parsifal* we find ourselves in the wooded regions in front of the Grail Castle. Before our eyes has passed the suffering of Amfortas, all the painful spasms of the 'wound which will not heal', the pain which always returns after the freshness of the forest's morning splendour lit up for a fleeting moment the 'night of pain'. From Gurnemanz's lips we hear the story of the Mystery of the Holy Grail, how once the heavenly hierarchies inclined to Titurel, wrestling in the struggle of faith during a holy night, how they bequeathed to his keeping the Holy Vessel in which Joseph of Arimathea received the Blood from the wounds of the Redeemer on the cross, and how Titurel built the sanctuary for the 'healing vessel', the Grail Temple, to which no sinner can find his way. We hear how Klingsor, who wrestles in vain for the holiness of the Grail, gained the forces of black magic through violating nature, how he became the adversary of the Grail, and how Amfortas, the son of Titurel, the announced Guardian of the Grail fell into the traps of the Grail adversary. No remedy could overcome the hot, consuming poison of the wound struck by the Spear. There was only *one* hope, the 'writing on the Holy Vessel' flashing out in the light of higher worlds revealed in a holy vision to Amfortas wrestling in prayer, the Mystery of the prophecy, 'Await him whom I have chosen, the simpleton without guile, made wise through compassion'.

The narration of Gurnemanz ends with this theme of the prophecy.[36]

Fig. 15

Whilst everyone on stage, deeply moved, repeats the words of the prophecy, a commotion occurs in the background; a wild swan, morally wounded from an arrow sinks to the ground in faint flight. Soon the archer, a youth, is brought forward—Parsifal who, thirsting for adventure, has run away from his anxious mother Herzeleide who longs for him. Led by destiny, he has now found his way to the Grail Castle at the very moment when the words concerning him are spoken. Parsifal is not in any way conscious of guilt, because he did not act out of actual ill-will, but only from natural joy and youthful enjoyment of hunting when he let fly the arrow, aware only of his marksmanship ('Whatever flies I can hit in flight'). The way he is reproached for his fault by the Grail Knights, especially Gurnemanz, is very characteristic of the whole spiritual atmosphere of the *Parsifal* drama:

> You could murder, here in the holy forest
> Where tranquil peace surrounded you?
> Did not the woodland beasts approach tamely
> And greet you innocently as friends?
> What did the birds sing to you from the branches?
> What harm did that faithful swan do to you?
> Seeking his mate, he flew up
> To circle with her over the lake,
> Which he hallowed so splendidly as a bathing place:
> It did not fill you with awe, but only enticed you
> To wild childish shooting with your bow?—
> He was our friend: What is he now to you?
> Here—look here!—here you struck him:
> The blood is still congealing, the wings drooping lifeless,
> The snowy plumage is stained dark—
> The eyes glazed—do you see his gaze?
> Now do you recognize your misdeed?
> *(Parsifal has followed Gurnemanz with growing emotion; now he breaks his bow and slings his arrows away.)*
> Say, lad, do you realize your great guilt?
> *(Parsifal passes his hand over his eyes.)*
> How could you commit this crime?
> *Parsifal*: I did not know (it was).

To illustrate this apparently everyday episode, the most sublime Grail-themes and Christ-themes already heard in the Prelude are brought in.[37] At the place 'the eyes glazed—do you see his gaze?', the *Gaze Motif* now appears significantly (as before with 'Here—look here!' and 'He was our friend'), in such a way that the up-rushing Parsifal-motif in 'youthful' B♭-major is suddenly interrupted by this 'Christ's Gaze Motif'.

(Parsifal has listened to Gurnemanz with growing emotion; now he breaks his bow and slings away his arrows.)

Fig. 16

Similarly, the previous crisis with '… but only enticed you to wild childish shooting with your bow?' (See Fig. 17):

And with 'Say, lad, do you realize your great guilt?' we even hear the *Christ's Passion Motif* itself above painful chords (see Fig. 18).

In *Tannhäuser*, *Tristan* and even in the tragically-serious *Twilight of the Gods*, Wagner depicts the hunting episode in a down-to-earth manner with merry sounds on the horns. Here, in *Parsifal* we see all the realms of Christ affected; the suffering of Christ Himself is connected with the suffering of the slain beast. No other episode shows so distinctly how much the *world of Parsifal* differs from the other dramas.

Fig. 17

Fig. 18

For in those we remain in the earthly-human sphere, whereas in *Parsifal*, however, we stand on the threshold of the spiritual world.

In the first Goetheanum at Dornach, near Basel, Switzerland, amongst the coloured-glass there was a *blue window*, reproduced in the second building visible today, which shows a huntsman shooting a bird. The situation before and after the deed is clearly set out in the composition of the picture—the exalted countenances of spiritual beings appear in the heights, their pained features expressing how the event is perceived in the spiritual world. Rudolf Steiner has given key-expression to all this: 'Man resolving. The outer world in resolution. He has willed.'

The picture on the window shows still more. We notice the twelve signs of the zodiac surrounding it in a solemn arrangement. As the Heaven's Holy Guardians, they look down upon the apparently insignificant, everyday occurrence of human life. They appear to admonish us:

> Take heed, child of man. Each deed you perform, including the most insignificant, or what appears to you insignificant, each thought, each word, each resolve, all must pass before the twelve Holy Guardians of the Heavens. You are only not conscious of this in the everyday world. However, when you cross the threshold of the spiritual world in death, or when you but come close to it during sleep, then all this stands before you, for you yourself suffer the pain there, which you have inflicted upon others. Everything arises here from within, from the innermost depths of your soul and whole being, and looks at you in a way that torments, in a punishing and judging manner. You have to give account of all that you have done, thought, felt and wanted!

The whole of the hunting episode with the swan in *Parsifal* is the same, right down into the smallest details, as the spiritual situation depicted in the blue window in the Goetheanum. The whole spiritual atmosphere of the *Parsifal* drama is explained through this as by nothing else. Here in the realm of the Grail Castle, before the threshold of the spiritual world, the hunting episode is no longer a childish, harmless adventure; what is called 'hunting joy' no longer expresses harmless natural enjoyment, no longer fun in the life of nature. In the very depths of man's own being the pain of the slain beast is felt.

What the Ancient Indian wished to express with the saying TAT TVAM ASI, 'Thou art that', comes to consciousness here as everything since the Fall of Man which exists as Archetypal Sin between the human and animal worlds, placed here before the soul out of the spiritual backcloth to life. In order that man could ascend upon the ladder of existence and could grow towards the stage of the ego, the human self, decreed for him by the divine world, the animals remained behind, sacrificed themselves. As brothers and sisters they stand *guilt-less* before the human being who has *become guilty* before the spiritual world. And man requites them all this, pays his debt by taking their lives for his enjoyment and consuming them. He does not know in his everyday consciousness that this is so. But in the realm of the Grail, before the threshold of the spiritual world, whether reached through death or by other ways, all this then rises up admonishingly from the depths of consciousness. *In all this man beholds the suffering of Christ crucified by him and within him.*

That is why in the music of *Parsifal*, where Gurnemanz reproaches the young Parsifal with his guilt, the Christ's Passion Motif appears, significantly connected with the *Gaze Motif*. In the glazed eye of the slain beast the eye of Christ looks, the gaze of Christ Himself beholds the culprit, who in childish folly is still not conscious of his guilt, who only feels an incomprehensible emotion in his heart when he is reproached. This whole episode with the swan takes place objectively in the spiritual world without its coming to the consciousness of the one who is involved in the process. Everything remains still in the *unconscious*, or in the deepest subconscious. 'The eyes glazed—do you see his gaze?'—even in the glazed eye of the slain beast is revealed the loving, suffering, reproachful gaze of Christ, which awakens confused torment in the heart. This is the first step of the dramatic development of the Christ-experience, the dramatic Christ-revelation in Wagner's *Parsifal*.

Scene 2. The Walk to the Grail Castle

In all seriousness the Grail Knights reproach the lad Parsifal with his guilt. Yet the fact remains that he has found the way to the Grail country, which is otherwise unapproachable for the sinful human being. Indeed, he appears there at the very moment when the prophecy about the Holy Grail is recalled, when the words of the prophecy 'the simpleton without guile, enlightened through compassion' was sounding solemnly on everyone's lips. Despite all that has happened, a connection must nevertheless exist between the mysterious lad, who does not yet know his own name, and this prophecy.

However, only in the temple, in the Grail sanctuary itself, can it be revealed how the spiritual world speaks to what is now revealed as a new thread in the web of destiny. For this reason Parsifal is now led into the Grail Castle as into the 'Temple of Trial'. Here it will be revealed whether, in the presence of the Holy Grail and with the suffering of Amfortas before him, he can be the one chosen to aid the Grail. A significant detail in this event is that no answer is given to his question, 'Who is the Grail?' 'That cannot be uttered in words, yet you yourself are chosen by it, if you remain faithful to the call.' To this Parsifal replies, 'I hardly tread—yet I fancy to have travelled far', answered by Gurnemanz, 'You see, my son, time here becomes space.' This happens while Gurnemanz and Parsifal walk together the way to the Grail Castle and the well-known Transformation Scene takes place, up to the passage 'Forest before the Grail Castle' (the Castle has arisen of its own accord), and finally we find ourselves within the Temple. The transition music accompanying this walk begins mystically quiet in A-major, the 'key of the loftiest heights' and of the distant Grail, sounding here appropriately with 'the sun stands high'. The music, by modulating into distant keys, indicates transitions of consciousness, to ever higher, mysterious, mystically-removed levels. All the time the quietly sounding progression of sixths from the well-known 'Awakening Call' (or 'Grail Castle Motif') conjures up at the same time the rising Castle before the external vision, the wakening ever more to consciousness before the inner vision.

With this a double aspect is indicated, in which everything can be understood. Within the outer event we behold at the same time an image for the spiritual. Without wanting exhaustively to explain the many-faceted Mystery of the Grail and its Castle, we could say that from a spiritual point of view, in this 'Walk to the Grail Castle' we step out of the earthly-spatial plane into another world, initially no longer spatial in the physical sense but basically a realm of occurrence in time. Steiner speaks of this world as the *etheric world*.[38]

We all know this crossing from the physically-spatial into the temporal-etheric in our daily passing from the world of everyday consciousness into that of sleep at night. The transition music leading from key to key paints this so expressively and meaningfully in the 'Walk to the Grail Castle'. We mostly sleep through these events because of this very condition of our consciousness. Nevertheless, looking at the experience of going to sleep can reveal to us the deepest mysteries of this walk to the Grail Castle in Act I, which we take as Scene 2, and illuminate its whole meaning. In this case it is a scene without the 'external' drama of words, apart from the few accompanying words already mentioned. It is a scene lying between the events enacted on stage during the transformation music, and the symphonic events taking place in the orchestra.[39]

The indication of the *experience of going to sleep* gives an important key to the experience within Parsifal's consciousness during the 'Walk to the Grail Castle'. That is not to say he actually falls asleep. Rather, his earlier state of consciousness as one of deep sleep, shown still in the swan episode, slowly begins now to lighten up. Consciously or unconsciously, Parsifal experiences what normally appears unconsciously while falling asleep each night.

The condition before we have completely entered the realm of slumber is well-known. Something like a confused resounding of the experiences of the day flutters, surges, and stirs around us. What we have experienced, thought, felt and done during the day arises in confused pictures, or like jumbled sounds, often in a way that becomes rather oppressive in our consciousness. A *judging element* is revealed in the human soul not only while crossing the 'threshold to the spiritual world' at death, but already in every approach to this threshold in sleep there lies such a 'judging experience', such a 'soul-crisis', even if it most of the time does not reach our consciousness—or only in a completely dull and confused manner. All our misdemeanours of the day, which often weigh upon our soul as a scarcely conscious self-criticism, rise before us in a judgemental and oppressive manner in those experiences during sleep.

Parsifal now lives through such a process in the 'Walk to the Grail Castle'. As he shot down the wild swan he wrought a deed which is regarded, according to the laws of the Grail country—that is, likewise before the spiritual world—as a deep sin. He was not aware of this guilt, and is even now a long way from understanding the meaning of that remonstrance. He has felt only an unclear, dull emotion in his heart.

What remains still concealed within everyday consciousness begins to arise, but now in a quiet, gradual 'waking up', in the 'Walk to the Grail Castle', in crossing over into higher stages of consciousness. Now we understand with the sudden change from piano to forte of the initial mystic-quiet and mysterious music, wandering through distant keys, the painful expression it acquires. And we understand the continuously re-appearing *progression of sixths* of the 'Awakening Call'—the motif of the rising castle and of inner awakening—suddenly coming against shrill tormenting discords.[40] This continues, until out of this whole development the *Gaze Motif*, the admonishing look of Christ emerges. This time not in a fleeting way as heard previously at the end of the Prelude and the swan episode—'eyes glazed—do you see his gaze?'—it towers up as a mighty symphonic movement. No word is spoken and no outer dramatic events occur; everything has become inner soul-drama.

What Parsifal did not yet recognize with his waking consciousness was the presence of spiritually objective facts, as in the glazed eyes of the slain animal the *Gaze of Christ* Himself—loving yet admonishing within the love. This fact is even now not fully conscious for him either; but it rises before his consciousness like a dim, confused echo of the day's experiences, anguishing, oppressive, arising as in the experience of falling asleep. Just as here we feel buffeted by a tossing ocean, so this *Motif of the Judging Gaze of Christ* is taken up and borne by the symphonic waves of the full orchestra, from the whole force of the strings and wind.

This is the second stage of the 'drama of the Christ-experience', which in this case is not expressed in outer drama, but in the pure symphonic element of the Wagnerian orchestra together with the transformation of the scene and its images.

(See Appendix I for the music to the episode referred to here.)

Scene 3: Amfortas and the Grail

The third stage of experience leads us now right into the Grail Castle, into the spiritual region itself, so to speak, in whose borderland we found ourselves up to now. Similarly, in Wolfram von Eschenbach's *Parzival*, the 'Wood before the Grail Castle' is the 'spiritual threshold', the solemn, destiny-laden borderland. Here in the inner realm of higher wakefulness and higher consciousness, Parsifal should show whether the forces of the heart ('made wise through compassion') can lead him to see *consciously* what happens there. This is the test which the Grail Knights present to him, as indeed they must according to the laws of the Grail.

Parsifal beholds the Mystery of the Holy Grail there—musically already indicated in the Prelude with the 'Transubstantiation'. It is the miracle of transformation, the renewal of the earthly forces in the blood. This event which historically took place uniquely on the cross of Golgotha works on further in the Earth's development. It is continually in the 'world of the Holy Grail', at that spiritual place only to be reached by the inmost opened member of the soul, the *consciousness-soul*. And it is this Mystery which is ever and again renewed, as the priest at the altar daily accomplishes afresh the transformation of bread and wine, mindful of Christ's deed.

However, between the Mystery of the Holy Grail and his soul, which should free the Mystery from the deepest forces of his heart, there is something else. Someone else stands in the midst: Amfortas, the sinful Guardian of the Grail, Amfortas who has lost the Grail Spear, the unconquerable *weapon of the 'I'*, *the self*, the unsurmountable *will within the 'I'*. He lost it to the adversary Klingsor, to the lord of the demonic forces in the blood, which oppose the pure redemptive effect of Christ's Blood, by awakening dark, destructive passion, all the hopeless suffering in the human blood.

Consequently, the unveiling of the Vessel bestowing blessing, the Grail celebration, leads Amfortas now to unheard-of soul-crisis and soul-torment. Here, too, the *Gaze Motif* is paramount. As the Holy Blood in the sacred Vessel glows crimson in super-earthly lustre, Amfortas sees the loving look of Christ dwelling upon him. He feels this 'sad, loving look', in which we saw the Prelude conclude. This gaze becomes a *judgement* for him, a crisis. It awakes torment in his heart, of which this motif always appears to speak. Amfortas feels the 'split of consciousness' as a tearing asunder. One side of his being deeply and inwardly experiences the Holy Mystery, the other side feels as though pulled down into an abyss of suffering and damnation.

Before Wagner could write out the poetry and music of *Parsifal*, he was inwardly occupied for a long time especially with this theme of Amfortas, already in 1859 when he was working on Act III of *Tristan and Isolde*. At that time he was already aware of the inner connection of Amfortas in *Parsifal*, of the sword wound inflicted by Melot in *Tristan*, with the spear wound in *Parsifal*. It is indeed basically the same, only the simple human element in *Tristan and Isolde* appears in *Parsifal* raised into the *universally human sphere*, into the sphere of Christ. Wagner writes of this in a letter to Mathilde Wesendonck (Lucerne, 30 May, 1859):

> All this quite recently set me again against Parsifal. It came to me again recently that this would be terribly hard work. Looked at closely, *Anfortas* is the centre point and main figure. But then this is not a bad story, this. Think for heaven's sake what's going on there! It became terribly clear to me. It is my Tristan of Act III unthinkably intensified. With the spear wound, and probably another one—in his heart, the poor fellow is in terrible pain knows no other longing than to die; to gain this highest comfort he longs again and again to behold the Grail, if this at least would close the wound for him, because everything else is indeed unable, noth- ing—nothing is able: the Grail, however, always gives him only the one thing back, just this, that he can NOT die; and because the very sight of it only increases his agonies by making them eternal. He has to long for his only comfort, for the blessing of the Blood which once flowed from the same spear wound of the Saviour, when He, renouncing the world, redeeming the world, suffering for the world, suffered on the cross! Blood for blood, wound for wound—but there and here, what an abyss between this blood, this wound! Completely transported, in total devotion, total

rapture, during the wondrous presence of the Vessel glowing crimson in mild, blissful light, a new life pours through him—and death cannot approach him! He lives, lives anew, and more terrible than ever the fatal wound burns in him, *His* wound! Devotion itself becomes agony for him! When will it end, where is redemption? Suffering of humankind continuing into eternity!—does he want to turn completely away from the Grail into the madness of despair, close his eyes to it? He wants this, in order to be able to die. But—he himself, he was ordered to be the Guardian of the Grail; and not a blind, external power ordered him to do that—no! because he was so worthy, because nobody else recognized deeply and inwardly the Mystery of the Grail as he did, still now his whole soul longs after all for the sight of it, which destroys him in his devotion, bestowing heavenly healing with eternal damnation!—[41]

What lay before Wagner's spirit as a world of abysmal conflicts and soul-tragedies is intensely concentrated in those two short musical monologues of suffering and outbreaks of pain in Acts I and III. These are in truth the prevalent soul-conflicts of our time. The human being of today—as Steiner once mentioned—is on the one hand a *suffering Amfortas* who cannot live and cannot die because the 'wound which will not heal' burns in his blood. At the same time, the human beings today are also the *seeking Parsifal*, who having gone or are still going through the nadir of materialism on the way to true knowledge, long and seek from the depths of the soul for the renewal and re-enlivening of the earthly sphere.

This great human experience, this great tragedy of humankind, is now placed before Parsifal at the same time as the Christ Mystery of the Holy Grail—this is the content of our Scene III. First, from the depths of the tomb, is heard the voice of Titurel, who is still kept alive through the grace of the Holy Grail, admonishing his son Amfortas to hold the Grail celebration once again. Then the despairing cry of Amfortas answers him, accompanied significantly by the *Gaze Motif* from the orchestra, 'Alas, woe is me! For my pain! O, my father, do you once again fulfil the office! Live, live—and let me die'.[42]

Behind the great outburst of Amfortas which follows on the repeated admonition of Titurel ('No! leave it uncovered! Oh! That no man, no man may undergo this torture awakened in me by the sight which transports you! What is this wound, its raging pain, compared to the misery, the torments of hell, to be condemned to this office! ...'), lies the soul-drama of the '*Gaze Motif*', as with the passage 'Oh punishment, punishment unparalleled, of, ah! The wronged Lord, bountiful in mercy!'

Fig. 19

Then, during the sounding of the 'transubstantiation music' from the Prelude, all the Grail events, the entire Mystery of the transformation and transfiguration in the radiant Blood of Christ are placed like a wondrous vision before the spirit of Amfortas. 'The divine contents of the Vessel glow with radiant glory', to which the following Klingsor motifs 'the ebb of my own sinful blood in mad tumult must surge back into me', create a grim contrast.

The music tells in an impressive manner, how all this reaches, should reach, could reach, the soul of Parsifal, how out of all this the sufferings of Christ himself, the stigmata of Christ, behold him. This climaxes for the whole music drama of *Parsifal* at the passage, 'here through the wound like his, struck by a blow from that same spear', where the cry of Christ's Passion sounds through the widths of space

Fig. 20

and where later on the expressive development of the 'Gaze Motif' connects with the 'Passion Motif' ('which pierced the Saviour, from whose wound the Holy One in holy longing of compassion wept tears of blood for man's disgrace'). One can feel the quintessence of the whole *Parsifal* music, the whole esoteric element of *Parsifal*, is contained in these few bars:

Fig. 21

All this penetrates into the soul of Parsifal. After the whole resistance of Amfortas has relapsed into a faint hope for redemption— again we hear the 'Gaze Motif' with altered nuances fade away within the 'Prophecy Motif' ('enlightened through compassion')—Parsifal has to behold how Amfortas, as if broken, walks with heavy, faltering steps towards the Unveiling of the Grail, which is forced upon him. Something like a 'revelation of humankind' lies here in the tired, as it were, staggering expression of the Christ's Passion Motif that precedes the Unveiling.

Fig. 22

Scene 4: The Gesture towards the Heart—Parsifal shakes his Head

We are still within the Temple sanctuary. The Grail celebration has passed before us, musically framed by the Last Supper Motifs which we recognize from the Prelude. The sequence of events is as follows (drawing on Wagner's own stage directions): While Amfortas in silent prayer devotedly bows before the chalice, an increasingly dark twilight extends over the hall. While the words of the Last Supper resound from the dome of the Grail Temple—heard purely instrumentally at the beginning of the Prelude as words of love spoken from cosmic heights, and appearing now as accompaniment to the sung words—a dazzling beam of light falls from above on the crystal chalice. This glows ever more strongly in brilliant crimson, shedding a gentle light on everything. Amfortas, with transfigured countenance, raises the Grail Cup aloft and turns it to every side. Everyone had already sunk to their knees when the twilight began, and now they raise their devout gaze to the Grail. The music here is an expressive development of the Motif of Christ's Gaze, connected with the Ego Motif of the Spear. Then Amfortas sets down the Grail Chalice, which now pales ever more, while the deep twilight disperses. At this, the acolytes replace the Chalice into the shrine and cover it as before. With the return of daylight, the cups on the table, now filled with wine, become visible again, and a loaf of bread lies beside each one. Everybody sits themselves down for the meal, as does Gurnemanz who keeps an empty place beside him and with a sign invites Parsifal to join in the meal. Parsifal, however, remains standing apart, motionless and silent, as if completely transported.

During the meal, in which Parsifal does not participate, Amfortas gradually relapses from his inspired exultation. He bows his head and holds his hand to the wound which starts to bleed again. Amfortas is carried out on his litter, and everyone leaves the hall in solemn procession, but for Gurnemanz and Parsifal who remain behind.

During the loudest cry of agony from Amfortas, Parsifal had made an abrupt gesture towards his heart, which he clutched convulsed for a long time. Now he stands motionless again, as if petrified.

Gurnemanz now steps ill-humouredly towards Parsifal and shakes him by the arm. Something is contained in this short event with which Act I closes; this is the particular reason we present it here as Scene 4. 'Do you know what you beheld there?' To this the stage direction reads: 'Parsifal presses his heart convulsively and then slightly shakes his head.'

A sacred Mystery has passed-by Parsifal who, through the marvellous guidance of destiny, has come to the realm of the Grail. He, the one called by the Grail, the one summoned to save the Grail, he had beheld all this with his eyes—the suffering of Amfortas, the suffering of humankind, the suffering of Christ; then in the glowing Grail the whole Christ-Mystery of transformation and transfiguration, and lastly, Amfortas 'suffering hopelessly returning ever again, the renewed bleeding of the wound'. In this *beholding* lies a process of consciousness. The gaze of Christ, the actual spiritual side of the event with the swan, still remains in his unconscious. With the 'Walk to the Grail Castle', he had experienced this spiritual event, this partaking of Christ, only as a dim, confused resonance—just as the events of the day sweep past us when we fall asleep—and now he has come to a higher spiritual vision in the inner realm of the Temple, in the *spirit realm*.

He beheld pictures of sublime divine-human enigmas. But his heart did not perceive their meaning. He fared as did the disciples, who spiritually led by Christ Himself beheld the Grail-experience of the 'Feeding of the Five Thousand' but could not reach an understanding of it because their 'heart was hardened' (as the AV/KJV well translates Mark 6:52, similarly Mark 8:17 after the other 'Feeding' where Christ directs the earnest question to the disciples: 'Perceive ye not yet, neither understand? Have ye your heart yet hardened?').

It was for a trial of knowledge that Parsifal was called to the Grail Temple. There he should prove to be the one chosen, 'made wise through compassion'. Before the Grail, however, before the spiritual world, no mere intellectual knowledge is valid any longer, no mere 'clairvoyant vision' which we have in the first instance in picture vision. Only what the heart speaks within man is valid. Only when the heart itself has become 'knowing' is the trial passed. In its deepest foundations the heart is indeed the organ of knowledge—*das 'an sich Wissende'*, the 'knower of the essence of things'—but through humankind's sin-laden fate this knowledge is as though buried. Only when the spell is broken, when 'the knots of the heart are loosened' as they say in India, when the 'hardening of the heart' vanishes, as the gospel language expressively puts it in this case, only then is the first step accomplished from mere external knowing or beholding to higher knowledge itself. Here, where the disciples of Christ failed in the Grail-Experience, Parsifal too initially fails.

The simpleton actually does possess the purest heart forces. But these forces are still slumbering, deeply hidden; they are not yet awakened. Parsifal, a mere youth, placed too early before the trial in the Temple, still carries a 'hardened heart' within him notwithstanding. The cry of suffering of Christ Himself within and behind Amfortas' cry of agony reaches him indeed in the dimly lit depths of his heart, which is why he clutches at his heart. The gentle stirring of compassion is present in his heart, but he has not yet been 'made wise through compassion'. The confused 'convulsion in the heart' is not yet loosened through heart-knowledge. So it is that his whole answer to Gurnemanz's question, 'Do you know what you beheld?' is again only a convulsive gesture towards the heart and a shaking of the head. He fails the trial of knowledge in the Temple; Parsifal is driven out from the Grail Castle, the realm of the Grail, with an angry gesture from Gurnemanz. 'So, you are just a simpleton then!—Off with you, be on your way! But heed Gurnemanz, in future leave the swans here in peace, and look for geese, you gander!' The 'way' which Gurnemanz means here is the pathway of further testing and chastising in the *outer* world—after the inner failure—the way which now lies before Parsifal according to his destiny. Upon him indeed the hope of the Grail still rests.

In seeking to lay hold of the meaning of these events we could say again, in that question of Gurnemanz, 'Do you know what you saw?' the eye of Christ, the loving, admonishing look of Christ Himself is directed towards Parsifal, questioning and searching, wishing to awaken the forces of the heart. Parsifal, however, does not understand. His heart remains silent.

All this, however, lies with eloquent distinctness in the music, in the way in which the *Gaze Motif* appears behind each of the 'seven scenes', dominating the whole Christ-drama of *Parsifal* in epigrammatic brevity and clarity, as here too, from a reminiscence of the motif 'made wise through compassion' accompanying the question of Gurnemanz himself:

(Parsifal presses his heart convulsively and then slightly shakes his head.)

Fig. 23

Scene 5: Parsifal in Klingsor's Realm: Awakening to Knowledge
After his failure in the trial of knowledge, Parsifal still remains the one chosen by the Grail. The 'way', which he himself does not seek and know at all consciously, *seeks him*, until, placed before new trials of knowledge, he seeks it ever more consciously, and going through many temptations and purifications, he eventually does find it.

So we meet him, who has been driven away from the Grail's realm at the end of Act I, now in Act II in Klingsor's territory that lies before the realm of the Grail. We were in the real spiritual realm there; here we are in that realm where those remain who possess *clairvoyance*, but do not yet reach to spiritual understanding of what is seen. If the realm of the etheric through which Parsifal travels on the 'way to the Grail Castle'—where time becomes space—reminds us of the experiential region of going to sleep, then the region where we meet him now is the 'region of dreams'.[43]

Many colourful flowers shoot up in this fantasy world of dreams, many with an intoxicating, even seductive fragrance. The whole region is full of blossoming charms, but also full of most serious temptation. When we keep this last fact in view we arrive at an ever clearer Imagination of *Klingsor's enchanted garden, of a garden of flowers* in which bewitching maidens grow, who dressed as flowers wish to entice everyone who enters this region.

The Prelude to Act II, so very different from that of Act I, storms past us, built up on those Klingsor motifs which we already met in the Amfortas scene of Act I. There they are the musical expression of all those demonic forces in the blood to which Amfortas succumbed as the sinful Guardian of the Grail, repeatedly overpowered and overwhelmed by their assaults. 'Klingsor's forces', the 'troops of Klingsor' are revealed in these demoniacal forces of the blood.

Prepared by the Prelude, in Scene I—to the meaning and context of which we shall return—we met the dark sorcerer Klingsor at work, through black magic drawing together all the threads of the net of temptation and enticement, which will now be placed before Parsifal. Then the floral splendour of the magic garden arises before us. We perceive Parsifal amidst the flower-decked maidens. His delight in the lovely flowers is a 'pure simpleton's' innocence of heart, their charming fragrance cannot entice him. Smilingly he turns back the maiden's coaxings to sport with love. But now the serious temptation draws near in Kundry, whom we know from Act I as the 'wild messenger of the Grail'. There her outer appearance took us aback, here in Klingsor's realm, however, we see her in a completely changed magical appearance, in enchanting beauty. It is the same temptress, to whose enticing charm Amfortas once succumbed, and who now is meant to try her art on the youthful Parsifal.

Who is this Kundry? Who is this strange 'temptress against her will', in whom Wagner has placed so expressively the whole demonic part of female nature? Wagner himself sought to solve the riddle of her being through the secret of 'repeated earth-lives', to which he was always attracted through his studies of Indian Buddhism—the letters to Mathilde Wesendonck provides evidence of this—until finally in *Parsifal* he included it significantly in the Christian sphere of consciousness of the 'Holy Grail'. Kundry's dark master, Klingsor, in the first scene of Act II, conjures her up through black-magic spells and makes her an instrument of his will. He speaks thus to the figure rising up phantom-like, 'Your master calls you, Nameless one, primeval witch Rose of hell! *You were Herodias*, and who else? Gundryggia there, Kundry here!'

Thus Wagner wants us to look for Kundry in one of her previous lives, in that dark sphere of perpetual hostility towards Christ and of the black-magic opposition to Christ, where the aim is to pit the dark magic of a demonic picture-world against the divine 'I', the will within the 'I' and the freedom within the 'I', which magic befogs, overpowers and overwhelms. We know this world of black-magic opposition to Christ from the Gospels. Especially from the part to do with Herodias in Matthew and Mark. We find it already in the Old Testament, where the Christ 'I'-Impulse has its great forerunner and pioneer in the cryptic figure of the prophet Elijah. In the dark couple Ahab and Isabel, we can sense a spiritual connection with the demoniac anti-Christian adversary incorporated later on in Herod and Herodias. We can feel how an opposition against the divine 'I' is involved here, deeply rooted in the depths of existence, carried through from life to life. In that world which later wants to realize anew the Christ-'I' Mystery from the depths of the consciousness-soul, the *world of the Holy Grail*, this opposition to the 'I' is incorporated in Klingsor, the black magician and dark adversary of the Grail. For Klingsor it is always most important to bring the unconquerable weapon of the 'I', the Grail Spear, within his power.

In this Klingsor receives help from the demonic side of the female nature incorporated in Kundry; she is the tool which he uses to trick the Grail Knight of the unconquerable Spear, the 'I'-weapon. In the sphere of Herodias—coming to life again in Klingsor's world—we shall thus look for Kundry, following Wagner's own suggestion.[44]

The unheard of did once come to pass. She met Christ-Jesus and laughed in his face. Then His gaze met hers, that gaze about which we repeatedly hear in the Christ-drama of *Parsifal*. Now she only knows *one* desire, to meet again the gaze of those eyes, in that look to find redemption. From life to life she carries this longing, rooted most profoundly in her heart. Here, however, the whole tragic destiny of this 'world demonic woman', as Wagner himself once called Kundry, is revealed. Her 'I', ensnared in the befogging consciousness of the dark mysteries, belongs to herself no longer. It has become forfeit and subject to the adversary. She must ever and again serve him who now stands before her as Klingsor,[45] as a tool for seduction. We see how she seeks through devoted sacrifice to the Holy Grail to do penance for that old wrong (karma)—and so we find her in Act I as the demonic 'wild rider' in the realm of the Grail, seeking in strange lands always in vain for new remedies for Amfortas—always in vain, for the hour repeatedly approaches when the opponent of the Grail, Klingsor, forces her to his will. He puts her to sleep through black-magic incantations as by remote control—violated by 'hypnotism', we would call it today. Then she suddenly mysteriously disappears from the Grail Knights, to reappear in Klingsor's magic domain, to cause fresh harm through renewed seduction. Thus Amfortas once fell prey to the charm of her infatuatingly lovely body—which she took on as a delusive form.

Act II begins with Klingsor sitting before his 'magic mirror', speaking dark spells into the sacrificial smoke of black magic, causing thus the figure of Kundry to arise. She is put into a frozen and cramped state of consciousness, to force upon her the role of the temptress against Parsifal. This scene clearly reveals that she actually does not want to play this temptress role at all. With the last remnants of her ego-consciousness, she struggles against the black magic, her strength of consciousness dwindling and sinking away. Finally, forced into the role of temptress, her further tragedy is that she no longer knows that she actually does not want to play this role at all, that her true self wants something quite different. Having now become entirely in thrall to the sorcerer, she completely gives herself up to the role of the temptress, quite possessed by the delusion that she could win salvation just in achieving the goal of this temptation. She hopes to meet the redeeming gaze of Christ in the eyes of her lover, to find in his arms absolution and healing.

As the dangerous one, the first temptress to be taken seriously in Klingsor's enchanted garden, she approaches the 'simpleton without guile', who smilingly easily rejected the enticements of the charming flower-girls. And we see in how refined a manner she begins her seduction.

Not only does she play with the false image of her external charm, but she aims to strike him at that vulnerable point in his heart, where the reproach of Christ weighs, resulting from the failed test in the Grail Temple. A dim remorse from an incomprehensible guilt quietly trembling in Parsifal's soul is sensed by her clairvoyant feeling. He has failed in just that power of compassion through which he could have become the helper and redeemer. And before the failure in the Grail Castle, another happened when he, without compassion, left his mother Herzeleide, who pining and grieving dies of a broken heart. Kundry now seeks to get hold of the 'pure simpleton' at this point.

As a sort of substitute she tries to ingratiate herself with her own 'loving embrace' where the memory of mother love and motherly affection still have a place in Parsifal's heart. She tries craftily to lead over the sublime, motherly aspect of womanhood into the other demonic-sensual aspect. And in the end it really happens that she, deceiving him with the illusion of a mother's kiss, presses a long kiss on to Parsifal's mouth, while in the music quite softly and significantly the consciousness-befogging Klingsor-motif appears.

In a way, Parsifal made one step towards the abyss after the temptation. It became apparent through this, too, how the adversary of humankind can befog consciousness since the Fall of Man in every person since there is some weak point in every soul. But stronger than the power of the adversary is the *connection with the Holy Grail* which remained with Parsifal throughout his experiences in his innermost being, and from there his innocence and purity of heart keeps him away from a final catastrophe.

Something completely different from what Kundry and Klingsor himself intended is released in him by this kiss. The one step taken towards the abyss, towards temptation, constitutes the actual 'Scene 5' in the experiential steps of consciousness unfolding in the *Parsifal* Christ-drama. This one, first delight from the fruit of the Tree of Knowledge occurring with the kiss, pulls up the 'simpleton without guile', so to speak, to *knowledge*. He could not be stripped of purity, who is chosen by the Grail, but the simplicity—and here we touch upon a deep Mystery—*is changed just in this first touch with the forces of evil, into knowledge.* Suddenly there arises again before him that picture which he had beheld in the Grail Temple, but which he could not yet understand in the depths of his heart, the whole picture of the suffering Amfortas in the presence of the Grail, with the hopelessly bleeding wound in which the whole 'wound of humankind' is revealed. He feels this in his own heart now; now the great crisis of humankind, present in everyone, has broken out in himself. 'Amfortas!—the wound! The wound! It burns in my heart!'

So we hear him, thus we see him now as if awoken through the touch of evil from a deeply dreaming state, as if jumping up in sudden shock, whilst in the music the *Gaze Motif* accompanies the outburst in grotesque form as though going headlong. We cannot stand before the great crisis of humankind, before the wound of humankind—felt burning in our own heart—without experiencing at the same time the *suffering of Christ over humankind* too in all this, without feeling the loving-reproachful, penetrating, judging gaze of Christ upon ourselves. For this reason the colossal, urging musical development of the Gaze Motif in what follows: 'Oh!—alas, alas! Fearful sorrow from the depths of my heart it cries aloud—Oh! Most wretched, most pitiable! I see the wound bleeding [here, too, the 'Christ's Suffering Motif'], now it bleeds in me!'

Fig. 24

And like Amfortas, Parsifal now experiences the sinfulness, the sense-infatuating fire in his own blood, while Klingsor Motifs are heard in the orchestra. The *suffering of Amfortas,* which he once beheld and yet did not experience with compassion, has seized him now as his own suffering. But with this, the other fact too is placed before him, which he met with once in the Grail Temple in connection with the suffering of Amfortas, the beholding of the Holy Grail itself, of the whole Mystery of the Holy Grail, the transformation and transfiguration of the Blood of Christ lighting up before him. 'My dull gaze is fixed on the Sacred Vessel'—here the Awakening Call, mentioned in Chapter I, is heard, which brings before the soul the Grail and the Grail Castle, causing it to arise in the awakening consciousness, reaching out into strange keys with visionary expression—

Fig. 25

'The Holy Blood glows: gentle, sacred bliss of redemption trembles through everyone's soul. But here in my heart the agony will not be stilled; I hear the Saviour's cry, the cry, ah! The cry surrounding the profaned sanctuary.'

The Gaze Motif in the orchestra gives utterance to his feelings, how he feels the *eye of Christ* directed towards him, how the gaze of Christ with all its redeeming bliss which it sheds, at the same time awakens agony in his heart. 'Redeem, rescue me from hands defiled by sin! Thus rang the divine lament in terrible clarity in my soul. And I? the simpleton, the coward, I fled to wild boyish deeds.' Notice during the words of the Saviour's agonized cry the transposition of the Last Supper Theme—or its beginning, the Love Motif—from A♭-major to the deeply painful A♭-minor, which always tells of the lost light.

So that one step towards evil, towards temptation and seduction, released in Parsifal the *crisis of self-knowledge* without which there can be no *knowledge of Christ.* It is the experience described by Rudolf

Steiner in his book *Knowledge of the Higher Worlds: How is it Achieved?* of the 'meeting with the Guardian of the Threshold' which is also placed before us here in the Christ-drama of *Parsifal*. 'Redeemer! Saviour! Lord of Grace! How can I, sinner, redeem my guilt?' So ends Parsifal's great dramatic outburst. It contains that breaking down of 'falling on the knees before the Christian cross', which once so deeply shocked Nietzsche about Wagner, which was something so terrible for him that he could not forgive his friend.

We observe here an intensification in the progress of Parsifal's consciousness in its whole development. On the one hand our Scene 5 bears the greatest resemblance to Scene 3, the suffering scene of Amfortas, how Parsifal experienced it in the Grail Temple with that sight which is then connected with the beholding of the Grail Mystery, the glowing chalice of Blood. Musically, too, the greatest similarity exists between the two episodes in the whole way the Gaze Motif, the Spear Motif, and the Klingsor Motifs are prominent therein, although in Act II everything is much grander, more urgent and more crushing than in Act I. The *enhancement of consciousness* lies in the fact that what remained in the Grail Temple as a *simple state of beholding, not yet laying hold*, what then could not yet awaken understanding participation in Parsifal's heart, is now raised to the stage of knowledge through compassion (*Mitleid*), through suffering it in himself (*Selbst-Miterleiden*), Parsifal now becomes in the highest sense *knowing*. That look of Christ, too, objectively there in the adventure with the slain swan, which lit up in a dull, confused way on the 'Walk to the Grail Castle', now reaches his consciousness, the spiritually conscious beholding of Christ's suffering has arisen out of pure spirit-vision, the self-renewing perceiving of the Grail events. And so the single episodes, steps or 'scenes' in the Christ-drama of *Parsifal* are mutually related. Is a further intensification possible? What follows will supply an answer to this.

Scene 6: Kundry-Herodias:[46] 'There His gaze fell upon me.'

We find ourselves in Act II at the dramatic climax of the great dispute between Parsifal and Kundry. Kundry is still as if possessed by the illusion of finding decisive redemption in the loving embrace of Parsifal. 'So it was my kiss that made you clairvoyant to the world? The full embrace of my love would raise you to Godhead!' she calls to Parsifal later at a point of highest dramatic intensity. After that kiss has released the awakening self-knowledge, the crisis of self-knowledge in Parsifal's vision of Amfortas and of the Grail, which released compassion in him, made him now *knowing*, the temptress sees only *one* more way to reach her goal. She tries to get hold of Parsifal just through his compassion, which all at once awoke[47] in him so powerfully and unexpectedly. This is her highest and last trump that she can now play against him. 'Oh, you cruel man! If you feel in your heart only the pains of others, now feel mine too! If you are a redeemer, what holds you back, evil one, from uniting with me for my salvation? Through eternities I await you, the saviour so late in coming, whom I once dared to revile.' So she identifies Parsifal with Christ Himself! 'Do you know the curse which through sleep and waking, through death and life, pain and laughter newly steeled to new affliction, endlessly torments me through this existence!'

Now we find as the actual Scene 6, the place which of all the appearances of the *Gaze Motif* is the most meaningful and effective both dramatically and musically, where into the whole false weaving—of solicitation and seduction—suddenly something like a glance from the world of truth shines in—even if Kundry uses what she thus places before her consciousness immediately as a means to new temptation—where Kundry herself speaks of the meeting with Christ in her earlier life, her Herodias-Salome incarnation. *'I saw Him—Him—and— laughed! … there His gaze fell upon me!'*

Fig. 26

Wherein lies the incredible enhancement of the drama and of consciousness when we regard this 'scene' in the sequence with the others? We observe that the *fact of Christ's gaze* is objectively present in some way in all those scenes and dramatic episodes. But the participation of consciousness is different and changes in each case. First, something with the slain swan at first remained totally in the unconscious. Next, what lit up only in a dull, confused way with the 'Walk to the Grail Castle', and then in the Grail Temple itself became actual *beholding*—in the scene in Act I. This passed over into the beholding consciousness of Parsifal but remained incomprehensible, also after Gurnemanz's question— this was 'Scene 4'—awoke only the vague pain in the heart, the 'spasm in the heart', giving rise to the mute 'gesture to the heart'. And finally, what returned after Kundry's kiss in Klingsor's magic realm returned as higher spiritual beholding, taken hold now at the stage of knowledge, shaken up to knowledge. All that led to this, that the beholding of Christ throughout all these events and crises, the *gaze from the eye of Christ* now becomes alive in Parsifal's consciousness as *spiritual vision*.

At first, however, present simply as spiritual vision. A further intensification is only possible when the meeting with Christ, which up till then still happened only in a one-sided way in the spiritual, is brought down now into the physical level. Wagner achieves this in an inspired manner through the dramatic turning point, where Kundry speaks of her meeting with Christ in her earlier life, '… *There His gaze fell upon me*'. Here the *gaze of Christ* remains no longer an unconscious or half-conscious spiritual event, also no longer as in the previous 'Scene 5' only a vision, but here this spiritually real event becomes *physically real* and *historical*. Here it is the gaze of Christ from the eye of Jesus of Nazareth Himself, the look of Christ who incarnated in Jesus of Nazareth, of Christ who walked the earth in Palestine, which the narration of Kundry conjures before us. It is the greatest dramatic moment in the whole of *Parsifal*, the inner core of the entire *Parsifal*-drama. The musical effect of the 'Gaze Motif' itself appears here at its actual climax. The reproachfulness in this motif, the *reproach of Christ* is evident at this point as at no other. And we feel, although the title 'Christ' might appear so often in writing throughout the ages, still we miss the actual reality of Christ behind the name. In this short dramatic episode in Act II of *Parsifal*, when Kundry tells of her destiny-laden meeting with Christ in an earlier life, in this 'There His gaze fell upon me', *the whole solemnity, the complete reality of the Christ-experience* is revealed as nowhere else.

(See Appendix II for the music of this episode.)

Scene 7: The Redeeming Gaze of Christ: *Karfreitagszauber*

Before we present the seventh and final scene, where the dramatic crisis of Act II finds its solution in Act III, we could briefly glance back to the end of Act II. After enticing Parsifal again by appealing to what for her is the only true healing, Kundry, definitively rejected, cursing now the ways of his redemption in wild uproar, calls Klingsor himself to help against Parsifal. Klingsor appears, and believes the game to be won, as in the case of Amfortas, but the Grail Spear cast from his hand is not able to reach the one who has remained pure and upright in the trial. The Spear rests hovering above Parsifal's head. Parsifal makes the sign of the cross with the regained Grail Spear. 'With this sign I banish your magic; as the Spear may close the wound which you made with it, may it crush your false splendour into mourning and ruin!'

With this the magic castle sinks into the earth as through an earthquake. The garden dries up into a desert, the girls lie upon the ground as withered flowers. The desert lies in the burning midday glare,[48] an expressive line of distant desolate mountains skirts the horizon.

At this point, with the collapse of Klingsor's false splendour, the motif which we called the 'Awakening Call' in the Prelude, striving upwards in a progression of sixths ends fortissimo in clear C-major over the 'catastrophic' F# in the bass. This motif reveals its full diatonic power within the surrounding chromaticism. It appears as the 'Motif of the Grail Castle' as the antithesis of the magic castle—which breaks to pieces upon it—as the 'Motif of Awakening Consciousness', as the antithesis of the quenching of consciousness, of the black-magic spell.

Parsifal, hurrying away, calls after the broken, screaming Kundry, 'You know where you can find me again.' Music in B-minor concludes this Act. What sounded in this key akin to Klingsor at the Act's opening has a completely different nuance in these concluding bars, almost reminiscent of the contrition in Bach's *B-minor Mass*. In these expressive bars in B-minor, a slight resounding of the Motif of Christ's Gaze, which so meaningfully controls the drama of the whole Act, mingles in, as though to say, 'You know where alone you can meet the gaze of that eye in which you will find redemption'. Therewith, the essence of the following Act III, 'Scene 7', is already indicated. Starting from the drama of the 'Gaze Motif', we could call this expressive ending of Act II 'Scene 7'; then the following concluding scene would become 'Scene 8'.

***

Although Act II lies very close in time to the first, between Acts II and III a much longer span of time is to be imagined, encompassing years, a long path of trials and purifications, struggles and sufferings through which Parsifal must still pass until he has become truly mature for the kingship of the Grail for which he is chosen. The ending of Act II, though, decided that he will reach this goal. The sign of manifold guilt still clings to him, however, and the stains received in Klingsor's realm in the contact with evil—which become for him the turning point to knowledge—have first to be cleansed before he can find the realm of the Grail again, from which he was once banished as the one who did not survive the trial.

All this is expressed musically in the *Prelude to Act III*, which has a more atonal character in contrast to the first Prelude, created out of its key. In this we perceive on the one hand the whole solemnity of the drawn out, thorny path of trials on which the goal, believed almost achieved, repeatedly disappears from view, seeming to dissolve into nothing, like a mirage—notice the characteristic quivering, rising, syncopated runs—and on the other hand, in the strong expression of faith in the 'prophecy' frequently sounding—'made wise through compassion, the simpleton without guile'. Yet above all this, we feel the positive assurance that the goal will be reached, that salvation and redemption beckon at the end of the path. The whole mood of this Prelude to Act III contains something of the successful overcoming of a serious illness, when in the still remaining fatigue a new and reassuring feeling of strength makes itself felt, when in the feeling of recovery something of soothing relief speaks, releasing previously difficult crises and tensions.

The Grail Castle lies before us again. Now a delicate mood of spring's commencement is present. It is Good Friday. On this day commemorating Golgotha, the return of Parsifal into the realm of the Grail is connected with the re-awakening of Kundry, found by Gurnemanz paralysed in the wild undergrowth.

After long wanderings and courses of trials, Parsifal has finally reached the goal. In black armour with closed visor and Spear held down, with bowed head as if wandering in a dream, we see him emerge from the wood. When taught by Gurnemanz the meaning of this place and of this holy day, he at last breaks the spell of a long silence. And in solemn emotion he reaches out for the hand of him who once expelled him from the Grail. 'Blessed am I that I find you again!' Now, before this greeting Parsifal had thrust the regained Spear into the ground and raised his devoted gaze to the Lance's point in silent prayer. Already at this moment the Motif of Christ's Gaze is heard, which we know from the first two Acts as the Motif of Soul-Crises, and which now with changed nuance, becomes the redeeming expression for beholding Christ.

In this sense especially, it appears at the dramatic climax of Act III which we place here as the final 'Scene 7'. As in the Gospel, Mary Magdalene washes the feet of the Lord, so here Kundry has washed Parsifal's feet at the holy well; the dust of the long wandering is taken from him. Parsifal, anointed by Gurnemanz as Grail King, turns to Kundry. 'My first office I thus perform: receive baptism and believe in the Redeemer!' It is the place, already mentioned in Chapter I above, where the 'Faith Motif' speaks of the 'chalice experience' with quiet and tender expression, of the 'lotus blossom of the heart' which now also unfolds in Kundry.

As in the Prelude, we can also see in the whole of *Parsifal* the characteristic construction of the drama, the interplay between the human and the divine worlds in the Mass. If in this sense, as discussed earlier, the end of Act III corresponds to the Communion, then the content of Act I with the Grail celebration and the Words spoken from the heights—the music of the Grail celebration is indeed the same as in the beginning of the Prelude—corresponds to the Proclamation of the Gospel. The dramatic content of Act II with the decisive crisis of knowledge, the turning of Parsifal towards the divine, corresponds to the Offertory. The beginning of Act III with all that is built up before us as 'Scene 7' is the equivalent of the Canon (Transubstantiation). The transformation and transfiguration, while it has deeply stirred Parsifal, Kundry and the realm of the Grail itself, spreads now in the holy hour over all nature, commemorating the Mystery of Golgotha. This is expressed from the very beginning, already in the Prelude.

In the whole solemn mood of Act III, the entire dramatic climax is reached in the *Karfreitagszauber* ('Good-Friday mood'), where, after the above-mentioned scene with Kundry, Parsifal turns and looks with tender rapture over fields and forest which now shine in the morning light, decked with the first delicate spring flowers. An event stood before Wagner's soul, which he at one time really did experience on a Good Friday, in the garden of the Wesendonck's villa overlooking the landscape of the Lake of Zurich.

A gentle breath of transformation and transfiguration lies over all nature in the first days of spring when, at Eastertide the rhythm of heaven and earth actually touch each other, coming to life in man, when for a fleeting moment—for all too soon the early blossom is followed by early wilting—the Earth itself seems to dream of her transformation and transfiguration in the distant future, of un-wilting, undying blossoms and fruits. As if the miracle of the Resurrection and transfiguration of Christ flowing from the Mystery of Golgotha wants to look at us for a moment from out of the opening flower chalices in the light of spring. In the entire music of the *Karfreitagszauber*, Wagner awakens for us the Mystery of transformation and transfiguration of all nature, from the first bars of B-major—where the accompanying figure expresses the tender swaying of the chalices in the spring light. It can be felt as something redeeming, striving towards the purely musical realm, after all the previous crises and their painful musical expression.

The actual drama of *Parsifal*—of which the Amfortas scene in the final part of Act III appears like a delayed Postlude, no longer quite current—has already there found its conclusion. The ending of *Parsifal*—with the 'Communion'—is no longer dramatic in the strict sense, but as Steiner[49] indicates, dissolves into Mystery-like symbolism.

The drama of this Act reaches its climax where Kundry, after receiving baptism, from Parsifal, sinks weeping at his feet; the 'Faith Motif' in its tender form of expression tells of the opening of the blossoms of the heart, of the inner chalice-experience. Compare the concluding words of the *Karfreitagszauber*, 'Thy tears become a dew of blessing, too; thou weepest—behold! The meadows rejoice', where the kiss which Parsifal gently presses on to Kundry's forehead appears in redeeming contrast to that other kiss in Act II. While Parsifal turns his gaze to forest and meadow, before the music of the *Karfreitagszauber* begins—which is taken from inwardly listening to the rocking and nodding of the flower chalices—something most meaningful occurs in those few bars creating a transition to the *Karfreitagszauber*, after the development of the Faith Motif. *Christ's Gaze Motif*, which has accompanied us through all the scenes and dramatic episodes of *Parsifal* and which is everywhere connected with the climax of this dramatic development, appears again here as the most momentous of all reminiscences of Wagner's entire music drama. It sounds almost in the same way as at the dramatic climax of Act II, 'There His gaze fell on me'. There:

Here:

Fig. 27

In Act II this motif paints the whole crisis, all the conflict within the soul. However, its expression is completely changed in Act III despite all external similarities, as though transformed to a purely redeeming expression, solving the most painful of all tensions. In Act II it leads into new issues, creating the transition to new desperate outbreaks of passion—also in the musical sphere—but now the mood of this motif, in which the gaze of Christ in some way always rests upon humans and the Earth, this motif now encapsulates the whole renewal of nature, absolved through the sacrificial death of Christ, and the whole life-stream of transformation and transfiguration. And this transformation and transfiguration of nature is intimately connected with the transformation of Kundry herself. This same gaze of Christ—so this motif seems to tell us now—which once in an earlier life awoke in Kundry's heart longing for redemption carried on from life to life, this gaze rests now as a redeeming one through the eye of Parsifal on her.

At last Kundry has found what she longed and sought for so hope-lessly through many lives. And all nature participates in this miracle of redemption. That is why, already within the *Karfreitagszauber* the Gaze Motif appears significantly yet again, where the creation is depicted, not able as the human being is, to behold Christ on the cross directly, and which consequently looks up towards the redeemed human being. The connection of the event of Golgotha with the transformation of the Earth and of humankind, already within the transformation section of the Prelude, finds here in the *Karfreitagszauber* in word and in music its clearest expression.

Appendix I

From Scene 2, The growth of the Gaze Motif in the transition music of Act I (The Walk to the Grail Castle)

Fig. 28

Fig. 29

Fig. 30

Fig. 31

Appendix II

From Scene 6, Kundry-Herodias: 'I looked at Him—and laughed ....'

Fig. 32

Fig. 33

Appendix III

Twilight of the Gods and Resurrection: Wagner's
Mythological Wisdom[50]

by Emil Bock

When Mathilde Wesendonck once called Wagner a 'wise man', in an answering letter he pointed out:

> But my child, what makes you see me, or want to see me, as a 'wise man'? I am in truth the most extravagant person imaginable. Compared to a wise man I immediately appear criminal, for the very reason that I know so much about this and that, and also know that wisdom is so much to be desired and is splendid ... I have such an awful lot of mythology in my head.

But it is only heartless, abstract wisdom which Wagner denied. Another statement from the Wesendonck letters shows that he felt he was the bearer of wisdom penetrating deep into the heart of existence, a clairvoyant wisdom:

> The tragedy of man lies only in this: If we all recognized the idea of the world and of existence at the same time and in common agreement, then tragedy and schism would be impossible. But whence this hubbub of religions, dogmas, opinions and perpetually warring viewpoints? It is because everybody wants the same, without recognizing it. Now the clairvoyant should rest with his faith, and above all—dispute no longer. He quietly endures the insanity grinning all around him. Only silence and sufferance help.

Wagner's mission was to announce and pioneer a new world-conception, perhaps more than to be a pioneer in the musical sphere. The foundation of his wisdom and the language he employed, however, was not that of abstract concepts, but of the pictorial world of myth. In this he admired and followed the Greeks:

> Their religion has nothing abstract about it. It is an unprecedented, sumptuous world of myths, which are all so formative and pregnant with meaning that you never forget their characters; and whoever rightly understands them finds the deepest world-conception hidden within

them. But they make poems and dramas of it and no dogma—totally artistic, deep and ingenious! A splendid people!

Wagner had no relationship to the ecclesiastical Christianity of his day, for he could not view pre-Christian religions as inferior paganism. The pictorial world of Teutonic mythology became for him a garment adorning the knowledge of Christ. His festive music-dramas are a grand Christian panorama, and in portraying this pictorial world he proclaimed a truly human wisdom.

The concept of the soul's redemption in Wagner's work has often been studied, but this idea too easily becomes superficial. Where do we find true redemption, for example, in the four dramas of *The Ring of the Nibelung*, in which everything is finally consumed in the world-conflagration? Where is redemption in *Tristan and Isolde*, when we are confronted with the Pietà-like figure at the conclusion—the dying Isolde holding the corpse of Tristan in her lap? Wagner's redemption is a deep, truly Christian one. Only through endless deaths and the great Fall into sin will humankind be ripe for redemption.

Wagner's great panorama both begins and ends with a meal—at the commencement of *The Ring*-cycle and at the conclusion of *Parsifal*. The food of the gods—the golden apples of Freia which grant them eternal youth—is lost through the Fall of Man. Humanity, who in the Grail Castle gathers around the Cup, is only sustained by grace, and must find redemption in the human food on the path from Valhalla's blessedness to the Grail Castle's solemn halls. This path leads through the deep 'valley of the shadow of death' [Ps. 23:4].

Through what power did destiny descend from blessed heights of light into the dark fatal depths? It is in the depths that the Ring is forged from the gold of the Rhine. Wagner did not intend abstract allegory with such images but uses them to express spiritual reality. The ring encloses, suggesting completeness and rest. When the human being attains an individual personality, he forges the Ring from the gold which lies on the river-bed. He learns to be strong in an individual self.

The longing to create the personality—the longing of the 'I'—was destined for the world, and so a curse disturbs the meal of the gods. For 'a rune of magic forces the gold into a ring. No one recognizes it, yet he who blessed love forswears can use the spell'. It is Lucifer-Loge who speaks these words. Individuality has been bought at the price of communion and love—unity in the old sense. The great descent of humanity from divine heights to the wasteland of death begins through the birth of egotism and selfish will. The twilight of the gods and humanity's dawn begin at the same moment.

The time comes when the gods feel the end approaching. Wotan chooses a human tribe on earth to receive the divinity which threatens to leave him. But the universal law is inexorable once the Ring has been forged, and the suffering of the gods' twilight overshadows human destiny. The childlike life of man changes, and so the brother and sister Siegmund and Sieglinde fall from blessedness and are cursed. The fall of the gods tears down humanity with it. Brünnhilde, daughter of the gods, wants to avert the dark curse from humanity, and in attempting this she also falls into sin. Wotan must punish his favourite daughter because she wanted to protect his favourite amongst human beings.

Only one hope for the future remains. Brünnhilde, surrounded by the wall of fire, is cast into a deep sleep. She is that single divine part which can remain pure. Will man one day be strong enough to arise from the wasteland of the Ring and gain the rock-summit? He must cross the trial-zone of the fire of desire, carrying the Ring. Then he may be united with the last daughter of the gods—the Eternal Feminine.

In childlike purity, Siegfried strides through the blaze and wins Brünnhilde as his bride. But once he has returned to the human realm, Kriemhilde upon Hagen's advice gives him a draught of forgetfulness. Man forgets the divine above the earthly realm, and the curse of the Ring works on. Instead of tearing himself away from the twilit world and ascending once again to divine heights, man drags the divine down into the earthly level in response to the curse of forgetfulness. The man of light is overwhelmed by the dark son of the depths. Hagen slays Siegfried, and Brünnhilde, unrecognized and degraded among earthly human beings, throws herself into the flames which consume Siegfried's corpse. The flames become a world-conflagration as the earthly world dies with the divine in humanity. Everything dies the great death.

Through the birth of individuality, man is expelled from Paradise, where Freia's apples bestowed immortality. The change of consciousness descends upon humanity. Finally the powers of the earthly depths stand upon the ruins as victors over the darlings of the gods.

* * *

The Earth becomes the scene of deepest suffering. Tristan fetches the bride for old King Marke. A magic potion causes a change of consciousness, and kindles the passionate fire of love in Tristan and Isolde. Tristan is faithless; he who fetches the bride for another desires the bride himself. Man can no longer selflessly serve the spirit.

The 'I', or self, is born. Man is no longer a selfless messenger, a pure and willing vessel to bear the divine on earth. The personal struggle for reunion with the divine begins. Man must learn what it is to be faithless in his striving for selfhood; he has to stand guilty before the regal Father.

At the beginning of Act III, Tristan (as the human being) lies mortally wounded on the walls of the castle in his homeland. Wagner originally wanted to allow Parsifal, wandering through the lands of the Earth, to approach Tristan's deathbed. To Wagner, Tristan was another Amfortas, because his wound is the wound of mankind. Isolde crosses the sea, but arrives only in time to see Tristan dying. She too dies, the grand 'death for love' (*Liebestod*). The night of death and deepest suffering reveals its most holy secret as Tristan and Isolde are reunited in death. King Marke rushes in to give Isolde her freedom because he recognizes that it was the magic potion and not infidelity which brought the lovers together, but he is too late.

King Marke, the bearer of the old, recognizing the evolution of world-destiny, prepared to sacrifice himself to the new. The past wants to give way selflessly to the future, as the father wants to give everything to the son. But the son is dead. This is the profound world-enigma. With the birth of individuality the time of the father passes over to the time of the son. But the initial fate of the son is death.

Wotan, the father, had to be angry with Brünnhilde because she wanted to protect the son, whose time had not yet arrived. But Wotan prepares Brünnhilde for the son who will one day appear. Marke wants to give the son to Isolde, but the son, Tristan, is dead in the arms of the dead Isolde. How can the son rise again to accept his inheritance?

* * *

A precise and intimate relationship develops both in the libretto and in the music of *Tristan and Isolde* and the *The Mastersingers*, but the one music drama is a complete reverse of the other. In the Prelude to Act III of *Tristan* the music is released into the sorrowful darkness of night. In the corresponding place in *The Mastersingers* festivity sounds: 'Wake up, day is approaching!'

If we look objectively at the story in *Mastersingers*, we can well ask: Isn't it nonsense that a singing competition for Eva the goldsmith's daughter should be held amongst the mastersingers where only one widower and one bachelor (Beckmesser) compete? The light-hearted and humorous play is not concerned with such questions. It celebrates the bearer of the new, and looks forward to the fresh, youthful life of the future. Hans Sachs the 'father' recognizes the true 'son' with unmixed feelings. He prepares for the new, playing God a little in roguishness and unselfish acquiescence; he 'pulls the strings of folly' till the desired result is accomplished—Walter's triumph over the old, pedantic Beckmesser.

In the wonderful 'folly' melody of Hans Sachs, Wagner expresses something of his deepest attitude to life—the profound divining and abnegating renunciation for a still unknown New. Wagner felt that the path to the New Age was to be found only through a deep renunciation, full of expectation. New-Testament wisdom finds its way into *The Mastersingers* in the humorous, light and genial openness to the world.

Hans Sachs has his name-day on John the Baptist's Day (Midsummer Day). He himself is like John the Baptist, who prepares the way for One greater, walking before the Son as a messenger of the Father. 'He must increase, but I must decrease' [John 3:20]. The message of the Baptist—'Change your thinking, the kingdom of heaven is at hand!' [Matt. 3:2]—is announced by Hans Sachs with the song 'Wake up, day is approaching!' Hans Sachs is the 'friend of the bridegroom'.

We touch upon Wagner's soul when we compare three pairs of figures: Wotan and Brünnhilde, Marke and Isolde, Hans Sachs and Eva. The father always struggles to surrender the succession. However, the depths must be reached before the son can begin to re-ascend; to begin with he is confronted by death. But Hans Sachs can open the gate of the morning. Where in the contemporary Church is the Christian enigma of the Fall of Man and Redemption, of the Father's sacrifice and the Resurrection of the Son, more vitally and strongly expressed than it is here?

* * *

After Siegfried has drunk the draught of forgetfulness and Tristan the love potion, redemption must manifest in the rise of a new light of consciousness. We turn now to the Grail poems *Lohengrin* and *Parsifal*. That Wagner wrote *Lohengrin* before all the other works discussed here is not important in this context.

Elsa of Brabant is freed from dark accusation by the Grail messenger sent from the gods: she will marry the deliverer but she must not ask his name. Nevertheless Elsa, entangled by dark powers, does put the forbidden question. And Lohengrin does reveal himself, but has to leave her. She gains the name but loses the living person.

Wagner himself expresses the meaning of the myth. 'I maintain that my *Lohengrin* ... sketches the deeply tragic situation of the present day, namely a desire for the spiritual heights, the longing to apprehend through feeling—a longing which modern reality cannot yet fulfil.'

An important reminder for modern humanity is woven into this story. Our thinking lives in the spiritual heights, but we are abstract. The human being asks the Elsa-question with his head. The human soul wants not only to be connected to the spirit, but to understand and lay hold of it as well. As long as Elsa does not ask, she has the reality. If she asks the question, however, the reality disappears. The curse of intellectualism confronts us.

In the way the human being today forms thoughts, he chases away the good spirits. Man knows an immeasurable amount, but his knowledge is limited to the names of the whole world and of himself, of God and of Christ. He is like Elsa after Lohengrin's departure.

And yet we know human beings have to ask; this overpowering longing lives deep within us. If we can learn to think with the heart instead of with the head; if we can learn to lay hold in feeling, then we are delivered from the tragic fate of Elsa. We become 'wise through feeling', a recurring theme in Wagner's philosophy. But 'modern reality cannot yet fulfil this deep longing', and so the Lohengrin-myth expresses 'the deeply tragic situation of the present day'. Will human beings ever fulfil this longing, and witness the sunrise of the new spirit-consciousness that does not drive away the spirit? Will the bridge be built between head and heart?

Here we arrive at Wagner's final Mystery-work, *Parsifal*. Parsifal treads a path upon which he will be 'made wise through compassion'; he arrives at the juncture where spirit is 'apprehended through feeling'.

We notice a mysterious theme of questioning in *Lohengrin* and *Parsifal*. Elsa may not ask, and because she does, the Grail messenger leaves her. Parsifal must awaken to ask, and because he does not, he has to leave the Grail Castle until he is mature enough to ask. This apparent contradiction is in actual fact a path of consciousness. The way has to be found from the Elsa-question to the Parsifal-question.

This process is the redemption of thinking. And this redemption is a most intimate concern of Christianity. If we set out to practise religious life only on a comfortable level and are able to leave out thinking as it is, we condemn ourselves to a Christianity only of 'names'. The true reality of Christianity only remains close to humanity when people learn to become 'wise through compassion'. Christianity without this wisdom is dead.

* * *

How is the breakthrough to the new era of consciousness in the human soul accomplished? How will true Christian knowledge be achieved? And how will the emptiness of abstract head-knowledge be enriched by a knowledge born of love from the divine-supersensory world? Wagner presents a Parsifal-path of four stages upon which Lance and Chalice are sought for and fought over.

Parsifal appears for the first time in the region of the Grail. The Knights reprimand him reproachfully over the sacred swan which he, the simpleton, has killed. 'Say, lad, do you realize your great guilt?' 'I did not know then.' 'Where are you from?' 'I do not know.' 'Who is your father?' 'I do not know.' 'Who sent you to seek this forest?' 'I do not know.' 'What name have you got?' 'I once had many, but now those names are all forgot' … 'Now speak! You cannot answer my questions; but tell what you can, for something you must remember.' 'I have a mother, Herzeleide her name!'

Through the restless wanderer, Kundry, Parsifal hears of the death of Herzeleide. Then he stands in the Grail Castle before the mortally wounded Amfortas who longs for death yet must always uncover the Grail which binds him anew to life. Grief, and with it the spiritual world, knocks three times at his still numb soul—the dead swan, the dead mother, and the sick King touch the simple soul like a dull throb. The human being feels the world-enigma but does not awaken to it.

Parsifal passes through the second stage in Klingsor's magic garden when he is tested by Kundry's temptation. In the realm of purification, evil kisses man in order to distract and fetter him. But beneath Kundry's kiss, the eye of Parsifal's soul opens. 'Amfortas! The Spear-wound! It burns here in my heart! … The wound I saw bleeding is bleeding now in me!' In the purification Parsifal wakes up to his own experience of humankind's wound. Kundry calls for Klingsor for help, and he throws at Parsifal the Holy Lance which he once stole from Amfortas. Parsifal, unwounded, is able to catch it. He wins individuality without falling into a destructive egotism.

\ Parsifal re-enters the region of the Grail with the Holy Lance. He meets the old Grail guardian, Gurnemanz, on Good Friday. The eye of Parsifal's soul opens still wider. He awakens not only to his own nature; the groaning of creation also reaches his heart. Death as the universal fate touches his awakened soul as he hears of the death of the ancient Grail King, Titurel. 'It is I who brought this woe on all!' The consecrated man becomes aware of a change. 'Today the fields and meadows seem so fair.' The Good-Friday music (*Karfreitagszauber*) radiates a gentleness from the heart of the earth. The earth is transformed into a shining monstrance. Gurnemanz draws attention to the miracle of transformation:

> Now all created things rejoice to see the Saviour's sign of grace, and raise a prayer to praise Him. Himself, the saviour crucified, they see not; and so they raise their eyes to man redeemed, the man set free from sin, set free from terror, by God's most loving sacrifice made pure. Today each blade and bloom upon the meadow knows well the foot of man will do no harm ... And, grateful, all creation sings, all things that bloom and pass away; nature has won her innocence, and all is renewed once more this day.

In the four steps of the Parsifal-path, Wagner presents in artistic images that same Mystery which is enacted at the altar in The Act of Consecration of Man of The Christian Community. The four stages of this Christian celebration of the Lord's Supper are the same as those through which Parsifal, made wise through compassion, becomes the regal bearer of Lance and Chalice. In the Proclamation of the Gospel, we enter the spiritual sphere, and the secret of the world envelops the soul like a cloud—in the biblical sense. In the Offertory, the soul has to step through the gate of purification, attaining its true potential through offering—the Grail Lance. In the Transubstantiation, the mood of Good Friday and the Resurrection flows out through all creation; bread and wine radiate in the light of renewed purity. And in the Communion, the human being, as bearer of the Cup, joins the sacred Round Table. The Sacrament, 'the medicine that makes whole', heals the wound of creation.

In the realm of traditional Christianity, two secrets of life in Christ have generally been forgotten, the secret of the Good-Friday mood (*Karfreitagszauber*) and the redemption of creation in the transubstantiation of the Eucharist, and the secret of working with Christ, knowing 'redemption is to the Redeemer', leaving behind all egotistical striving for redemption. Christianity has drunk a draught of forgetfulness, has lost its own sacramental and cosmic nature along with its wisdom. Wagner endeavoured to offer the antidote—the draught of remembrance. And many people who find sacramental Christianity strange, or who completely reject it, behold with open souls the images of transformation Wagner presents on the stage. Will the draught of remembrance have any influence? The altars of The Christian Community are raised in the conviction that now is the time to recall the Mysteries of Christianity, not only in artistic images but as real sacramental events in the world. Resurrection is to succeed the twilight of the gods.

Appendix IV

King Ludwig II of Bavaria
on the 70[51] anniversary of his death

by Rudolf Frieling

It was on 13 June 1886, on a dull and rainy Whit Sunday, that the strange life of King Ludwig II come to a tragic end in the waters of Lake Starnberg. The King, who had his authority taken from him on account of his 'paranoia', had arrived at Berg Castle on the previous day after an eight-hour coach journey. The Castle had been converted into a mental institution with peep-holes in the doors, which could not be opened from the inside. Dr Gudden, the psychiatric authority, had seized the King without prior examination in his remote Neuschwanstein Castle on account of 'misleading reports on paper'.

Dr Gudden was pleased to telegraph to Munich, that 'everything is running well according to plan'. But the doctor was quite mistaken about the patient's inner reaction. The King did suffer, without doubt, from a disturbed mind, but he was sane enough to feel this humiliating treatment with all his soul. On Sunday, during a lull in the rainstorm, the doctor even risked walking alone with the King in the park along the lake. What happened then—whether the King's death was suicide, or due to a heart attack resulting from an attempt to escape by swimming, cannot be made out for certain.

The bodies of the two men were found in the water when it was already dusk. It was apparent that the doctor had tried to restrain the King from taking his 'road to freedom' by the one way or the other. Resuscitation, attempted in the flickering lights of storm-lanterns, was given up around midnight, and the bodies were taken to Berg Castle by boat.

Ludwig II was one of the great 'non-contemporaries' of his century. 'Poor me; to have landed in such a century', he wrote about himself (in a letter of July 1871). But we recognize that even non-contemporaries have an important task to fulfil in preventing their fellow humans from completely losing themselves in new ways, in reminding them of values other than the material. Sometimes in the apparent nostalgia for things long passed, there lies hidden a hint of what will come; for the true values of the past will reappear in different form for future times.

Ludwig II was often called the 'fairy-tale king'. He rode by night in a golden shell-like sledge drawn by six white horses through the snowy forests and in the mountain valleys of Upper Bavaria. If the people of his country loved him in their special way, it was not for his achievements as a ruler or for his love of the people. He was distant and shy, although he sometimes showed himself to be generous and helpful to simple folk in Upper Bavaria. But he retained a splendour in the grey reality of a dull century, a last splendid echo of a lost fairy-tale world.

From childhood on, Ludwig lived in a fairy-tale picture-world. Fate would have it that he spent a long span of his childhood in Hohenschwangau Castle, near to the place where he later had Neuschwanstein Castle built. For Ludwig this south-west corner of Bavaria was always associated with the motif of the swan. The place-names reflect this—there is a village there called Schwangau, and the lake is named Schwan See. Also, a twelfth-century castle was built by the Schwanstein family. During that time the saga of the Knight of the Swan was still alive in popular consciousness of the people.

Lohengrin, the Knight of the Swan, was a son of Parsifal. Parsifal's secret of the Holy Grail was the focus of an underground Christian movement which worked against the official Roman Church by attempting to lay the foundations for a future Christendom of the Holy Spirit. It was not without purpose that King Arthur held his Round Table at Whitsun (Pentecost)—the feast of the Holy Spirit—and it is said that the Knights of the Holy Grail received their orders on the Saturday before Whitsun.

It was in Hohenschwangau that the young Ludwig saw the romantic frescos which were painted in 1836. These included scenes of Lohengrin's farewell from the Grail Castle, the Emperor hearing the horn of the approaching Knight of the Swan, and the fight for Elsa, and finally Lohengrin's wedding. When the young lad was not living at Hohenschwangau, he brought with him an album of these pictures to admire. Included in one of his childhood wishing-lists is 'a picture of the Knight of the Swan'.

The young boy lived in this legendary world as if it were real. It is said that his teacher once found him sitting alone in the dark at night, and suggested he have a story read to him so as not to squander time aimlessly. The boy replied, 'I am not at all bored; I dream up beautiful things and this pleases me.'

In 1856 the opera *Lohengrin*, by a certain Richard Wagner, was performed for the first time. Thirteen-year-old Ludwig was not yet allowed to visit the theatre, but his understanding governess told him all about it, and he was very enthusiastic. Finally, the time came when he was allowed to attend a performance of *Lohengrin*. The not quite sixteen-year-old youth was deeply moved, and shed bitter tears. Three years after this he was summoned from Hohenschwangau to Munich to attend the deathbed of his father. He was crowned King on 10 March 1864. Only five weeks later, his cabinet secretary went to Vienna to seek out Wagner, as it was the young King's warmest wish to meet him.

The search turned out to be difficult, as the composer was fleeing from his creditors. His desperate wandering had already taken him to Munich on 25 March—Good Friday. One year later, Wagner writes:

> Last year I spent Good Friday in Munich as an escape. I was travelling … unfit and suffering … I strolled along some streets of the city. The weather was rough and miserable … In a side street I saw in the window of an art shop a painting of the youthful successor of the monarch who had just passed away. I was captivated by the immense charm of his unbelievable soulful features. I sighed to myself, 'If he were not the King, wouldn't you like to get to know him' … I walked on lonely and in silence … It was more wonderful than a poet could describe. Indeed! He found me.

Finally, Ludwig's messenger came upon him in Stuttgart. He presented Wagner with a portrait of the King and a ruby ring. 'As this ruby glows, so will Ludwig, after the meeting with *Lohengrin*'s poet of musical sound.'

A few weeks earlier, it so happened that Ludwig had attended another performance of *Lohengrin*. So the two met in the sign of the Knight of the Swan on 4 May, 1864. They both felt the deep fatefulness of the meeting. For Wagner, who was then fifty-one, it came as a salvation from the brink of disaster—a true miracle at the last moment. He had written just shortly before, 'A light has to shine from somewhere. Somebody has to appear who can help effectively … A truly helpful miracle must occur now, otherwise everything is finished.'

The King made it possible most generously for Wagner to pay his debts. For this purpose Wagner travelled once more to Vienna, and then moved into a villa by Lake Starnberg, near Munich, by the middle of May. During those same days Ludwig also moved into Berg Castle [also by Lake Starnberg]. On 16 May (it was Pentecost) their wonderful spiritual exchange was renewed. Wagner speaks of a 'deeply fatalistic liking' and once called Ludwig his 'brotherly son'.

> He understands and knows everything of my soul ... Unfortunately, he is so beautiful and inspired, soulful and magnificent, that I fear his life must dissolve like a fleeting dream of the gods in the common world ... If only he lives on, it would be such an extraordinary miracle ... It is a most touching relationship. This thirst for knowledge, such understanding, such trembling and kindling ... A disciple has come down from heaven, destined for me. He knows and understands me through revelation, as no other being does ... Lord, that I should experience this, Master and disciple! And what a disciple!

Wagner regarded the fact that Ludwig was born at the same time he was writing his first draft of *Lohengrin* as a significant stroke of destiny. It was the important summer of 1845, when Wagner made the acquaintance of Wolfram's epic *Parzival*. At the age of thirty-three the world of the Holy Grail had opened to him for the first time. A magnificent spell lay over these happy weeks in the true spirit of Pentecost (Whitsuntide).

The relationship could not always continue like this. Shadows crept over even this union of minds. But what came between them did not drive them apart for any length of time. It is worth noting that the King, whose mind was so complex, remained loyal to Wagner until the very end, and despite temporary estrangements rescued him repeatedly with royal generosity to make his life's work possible. Wagner's desperate cry from the year 1867, 'For God's sake let us save the best of our relationship' was heard by destiny after all.

The King became engaged to his cousin Sophie, sister of the Empress Elisabeth of Austria, in 1867. In his letter of congratulations, Wagner finds the name of the bride to be significant. He speaks of a deep subconscious spiritual need motivating us when making our vital decisions. Now 'it' itself has spoken to him out of the deepest secret of all eternity! '*Sophia*—wisdom—of love!' He had chosen well, Ludwig, who was still completely engrossed in *Lohengrin*, calls his bride-to-be 'Elsa'. But just as there was doom hanging over Lohengrin and Elsa, so the engagement to Sophie did not lead to marriage, for they separated that year. Later on, Sophie died in a fire at a charity bazaar in Paris.

Once the King wrote these strange words to Sophie:

> You know the nature of my fate. I wrote to you once from Berg about
> mission in life. You know that I do not have many more years to live,
> and that I shall leave this earth when the terrible moment comes—when
> my star has ceased to shine and when he [referring to Wagner] has gone.

Prophetic words! Ludwig was to outlive his master by only three-and-a-half years. In these last years he slid away into an unreal world to an increasing degree; his true self seemed already very distant and no longer quite on this earth. It seems that the friendship with Wagner helped the King to be strong in his true being. When Wagner finally departed, he was left with no inner stability as support.

* * *

The shadows of Ludwig's mind and soul were surely present before Wagner's death. His spiritual picture-world, a divining of the Grail, could not find its way into his full, clear consciousness, and in place of a healthy spiritually-enriched consciousness, the mental illness or 'madness' developed as a negative force. This is why so many of the King's actions bear the nature of caricature. Ludwig's architectural initiatives in particular have been criticized.

Neuschwanstein Castle was built as a kind of crown for the old Hohenschwangau. It was in this castle that the picture-world of Wagner's entire music dramas was to find its glorification; naturally once more emphasizing Lohengrin and the swan motifs. The throne-room is of Byzantine style, with heaven and earth above, and the golden sun and stars depicted on a blue background below. The floor is a graceful mosaic of plants and animals, illustrating the mediation between the world of angels and the world on a gold background. The throne itself, to which nine marble steps were to lead, was incomplete at Ludwig's death, as was the Palace. But a great deal is revealed to us here—a kind of idea in Ludwig's soul of a cosmically-orientated Divine Right of Kings.

Ludwig's Palaces of Linderhof and Herrenchiemsee were inspired by this cult, which was the same as that of the Bourbon Ludwigs and especially the 'Sun King', Louis XIV. The 'Sun Kingdom' of that absolute ruler, however, was in reality no more than a caricature of a Sun Kingdom to be understood much more deeply and spiritually. In his subconscious search for a cosmic picture-wisdom taken from ancient times, Ludwig 'misguidedly' involved himself in this Bourbon solar cult.

In these palaces the peacock reigns instead of the swan. Medieval pictures show the various forms of consciousness symbolized in the shapes of four birds: raven, peacock, swan, and pelican. The raven brings word but is itself still doomed to ignorance. The peacock unfolds its miraculously colourful fan—the picture-world of 'Imagination'. The swan signifies Inspiration, for the miraculous music which fills the silence with premonition. In German there is an expression *'Mir schwant etwas'* ['I sense, have a premonition, of what might happen']. And we speak of a 'swan-song'. Finally, the pelican—who according to legend opens its breast to nourish its young with its own heart's blood—represents the highest level of Intuitive communication of being. If these pictures are not taken symbolically, however, but as the real thing, and if someone gets caught in them, they become meaningless and 'vain'. In the richly decorated palaces, Ludwig wanted to pay homage to the peacock and did not quite steer clear of this fatal rock, where the real image is replaced by vain unreality. One must have experienced Herrenchiemsee Palace illuminated by night, where thousands of candles shine in the vast gallery of mirrors, to sense the dream-world where the King's lonely spirit-thirsty soul had trapped itself.

We could also speak of a moon-cult practised by the King. His soul could not drink enough of the magical moonlight by the lake, in the mountains. More and more the day became night to him. This disease of a mentally ill person could also be interpreted as a longing for cosmic experience to transcend the barren, empty consciousness of the day.

* * *

After a lengthy separation, the King and Wagner met again in 1876 when *The Ring* was performed in Bayreuth. (Even 'Bayreuth' would never have existed without Ludwig's generous aid.) Ludwig's shyness with crowds had already progressed so far that he got off the royal train at midnight at some signal box to escape the ovations of the crowds. During these years something like a second flowering of the friendship occurred. This time it was not so much *Lohengrin* but the other Grail drama, *Parsifal*, which brought them closer.

After Wagner had read Wolfram von Eschenbach for the first time in 1845, the idea of *Parsifal* re-awakened in his soul in April, 1857, after his well-known Good-Friday experience, which he felt was the actual moment of conception of his *Parsifal*-creation. In the already-mentioned letter of April 1865, where he describes how as a fugitive in Munich he saw the painting of Ludwig, he writes:

> Today is Good Friday once again! Oh, holy day, the most significant day of the whole world! A warm, sunny Good Friday inspired me to *Parsifal* by its holy mood. Since then it lives on in me and flourishes like a child within its mother's womb. With every passing Good Friday it matures by one year, and I celebrate from the day of its conception to the day of birth which is to follow ... Even in all my sadness then, I still celebrate the day of the conception of my *Parsifal* on that Good Friday—indeed the painting in that tiny street unintentionally led me to my hero once again. The young King and Parsifal become one.

In the summer of 1865, Wagner writes in his diary, 'The King asks desperately to hear *Parsifal*—how wonderful'. He felt this longing to be a signal, just like a call of destiny. The following day Wagner already sat at his desk and put the first detailed prose layout of the *Parsifal* text to paper. He sent the final draft to Ludwig with the question, 'Is it good?' Ludwig replies enthusiastically, 'How I was moved by the script! ... I am forced to think continuously of *Parsifal*. I am burning for it. *Tristan* was born, and *Parsifal* has to be, too ...' It is not idle talk or flattery when Wagner names the King as the 'directly participating partner, the joint-creator' of his *Parsifal*.

At last, in July, 1877, Wagner was able to send the completed poem to the King. Ludwig writes, 'My mood, when sinking into the wonderfully soulful and elating poetry, can only be compared to the rapture that filled me when I received my first Holy Communion, so sacred, so pure'.

Ludwig had a hermitage built near Linderhof Palace similar to the Gurnemanz-hut and hoped to relive the Good-Friday mood there. He did not tire of urging the master to complete the musical composition. 'Do not forget, I beg of you, here's to *Parsifal*!' [Good Friday, 1880].

In November, 1880, the work is sufficiently completed for Wagner to present the Prelude to the King in Munich. Earlier, on 10 November, he attended with the King a private performance of *Lohengrin*. This too seemed like a stroke of destiny, that the two were able again to experience *Lohengrin*, which originally had brought them together, for after November 1880 they were not to see one another again on this earth. On the afternoon of 12 November, Wagner conducted the Prelude to *Parsifal* with the King as the only audience, after having prepared for him a short written explanation in which the inner motifs of the

Prelude are outlined as 'love—faith—hope'. At Ludwig's request, the Prelude was repeated … Even that was not enough, for the King insisted on hearing the Prelude to *Lohengrin* 'as a comparison'. This was felt as an unfeeling imposition by Wagner, who is said to have been very annoyed. Despite that, we would agree with Werner Richter, who in his book[52] about Ludwig says:

> But do we know that Ludwig did not feel that the fateful union with Wagner was nearing its end? Was it not because of that that he asked for the sounds, which had started it all, when the youthful Prince, filled with tears, heard *Lohengrin* for the first time, in order to look it over in its entirety with his 'inner eye'.

Even if Wagner was cross then, he overcame it quite quickly. Already on 14 November, he wrote, 'And so, the autumn of my life became once more a spring May Festival of my life'. He remembered again the Whit Sunday of 1864. 'I feel as if I have become quite young again.' And Ludwig, in his hermitage, engrossed himself with the explanations which were given to him for the Prelude; but when—in July and August of 1882—the completed *Parsifal* had been repeatedly performed in Bayreuth (sixteen times), Ludwig caused the master a deep and painful disappointment. He did not come. Wagner commented: 'No blow could strike so hard—who encouraged me to this mammoth last effort of all my spiritual strength? In retrospect—for whom did I carry all this out?' He felt his death was approaching.

The King was unable to conquer his shyness of crowds, and in his last letter to Wagner he expresses his hope of a private performance in Munich in the spring. He conveys a delicate understanding of the right season when he suggests that *Parsifal* ought not to be performed in July or August but in spring instead, the season when the deed of Golgotha is remembered. In Wagner's last letter to Ludwig, *Parsifal* is mentioned once more. The letter closes with these words, 'So I shall close the circle of my existence with the memory of the noble favours, in the enjoyment of which I am dying'. Wagner died soon after on 13 February, 1883. Ludwig was indeed entitled to say, 'The artist whom the entire world is mourning was first recognized by me, was saved for the world by me!'

But the circle of his existence too was closing fast. In June 1886, Dr Gudden signed the document. An initial attempt to overpower the King failed due to the loyalty of the country folk towards him. Ludwig was thus granted a short interval, which he was not able to utilize. During the last day and night he wandered restlessly through the rooms of Neuschwanstein Castle. The rain was falling constantly and even Whit Sunday dawned to a grey sky. After midnight the commission arrived and, as morning broke, the carriage with the King as prisoner left the Castle courtyard. Where the road turned he wiped clear the steamed-up window to cast a last glance at the Castle, which he had built for his swan drama.

His true and real being was kindled during the relationship with Wagner, but this could no longer penetrate the earthly shell, overshadowed as it was by illness. But this actual being did intervene once more, as it were from beyond, and directed the act of his death to Whit Sunday. The ill Ludwig is not the real person, he is 'maya', but in his last gesture of destiny, his true reality was revealed.

HERMANN BECKH

Orientalist, University Lecturer, Co-founder of The Christian Community, Independent scholar[53]

* 04-05-1875 D-Nuremberg
† 01-03-1937 D-Stuttgart
by Gundhild Kačer-Bock (Beckh's biographer, d. 2008)

HERMANN BECKH, as a cultural researcher, exponent and lecturer, belongs to the exceptional figures of the Anthroposophical Movement before World War II.

He was the son of Eugen Beckh, co-owner of a factory for metal thread; his mother Marie, née Seiler [outlived her son]. His sister was twelve years his junior, to whom he was closely connected—she died already in 1929. Beckh grew up in a prosperous, sheltered situation. He was a highly gifted yet sensitive child, who possessed a fine ability to differentiate colours, musical sounds and moods of nature. At five years old in the mountains, which he greatly loved all his life, he experienced a body-free condition that convinced him that human beings live through a pre-existent existence in the supersensory world.

At school it was apparent the he possessed an exceptional memory. The teaching methods put him off all subjects so that he could not decide on a profession. Nevertheless, a brilliant *Abitur* [school finals] earned him a scholarship to the Maximilianeum in Munich, where in particular the future members of the Civil Service studied. His original plan was to study national economics, because he hoped in this subject to be able to work for the social development of humanity. Through his fellow students he was increasingly stimulated to study law—he became by chance a judge, without a real decision to enter this profession, as he himself said. He ended his studies with his prize-winning work on *Die Beweislast nach dem Bürgerlichen Gesetzbuch* ['The onus of proof according to the code of civil law'], but practising as a judge he soon saw that it was impossible for him to be a judge all his life, when he actually wanted to help human needs. So at that moment when he stood directly before a position in the Civil Service, he broke from this professional path and began again from scratch. He began to study Indian and Tibetan philology, was promoted to Berlin in 1907 with his work on Kalidasa's 'Meghaduta' ('The Cloud Messenger'). With his inaugural dissertation a year later with a further work on this text, he became one of the few specialists in the Tibetan language to teach at the University of Berlin and worked on the manuscripts in the *Königlichen Bibliothek* (Royal Library).

In 14 December 1911 Beckh heard for the first time a public lecture by Rudolf Steiner (on the prophet Elijah; in GA 61. 194-220). From then on he concerned himself intensively with Rudolf Steiner's basic books. After a personal conversation with him, he became a member at Christmas 1912 of the Anthroposophical Society. A few weeks after Rudolf Steiner admitted him to the Esoteric School. During the course of 1913 he experienced a decisive climax in Steiner's career. In February the first Annual General Meeting of the newly-founded Anthroposophical Society, in August the Munich Summer Conference with Rudolf Steiner's Third and Fourth Mystery Dramas, the very first eurythmy performance, Rudolf Steiner's lecture as well as the Christmas lecture-cycle in Leipzig on *Christ and the Spiritual World* (GA 149), through which he received important impulses for the development of a renewed study of the stars. Despite the War, at Easter 1915 he could spend some days in Dornach and perceived the progress of the building of the Goetheanum.

In 1916 Beckh was called up for War-service. Shortly before the two small volumes of *Buddha und seine Lehre* in the Göschen series were published [Eng. ed. *Buddha's Life and Teaching,* TL 2019]—the climax and in a certain sense also the end of his academic activities. First he was sent to the Balkans, after which he was called to the *Institut für Seeverkehr und Weltwirtschaft* [Institute for Shipping and World Economics] in Kiel, where he had to evaluate the economic articles in the Scandinavian Newspapers. For this he had to learn the Scandinavian languages, so that he had now mastered English, French, Italian, and the Scandinavian languages, along with Greek, Latin, Hebrew, Egyptian, Syrian, Sanskrit, Tibetan and Old Persian (the language of the *Avesta*). His War-service responsibilities—from August 1918 in the Berlin Foreign Service—lasted into the post-War period.

Alongside this he began again to lecture in the University of Berlin. However, he saw that his professional future no longer lay in this realm, so he searched for a possibility to work for the future of human development. He gave up his teaching post for Tibetan philology and went on leave from the University. When an extension of his leave was denied, and instead of becoming a Professor without a Chair, in November 1921 he wrote to have his name withdrawn from the list of private tutors. This was the end of his academic career.

Already in 1920 Beckh offered himself as an anthroposophical lecturer. He gave lectures on linguistics at the Anthroposophical Conference of 1921 and in March 1922 at the Berlin Conference, where he led the day on [*Sprachwissenschaft*] philology under the theme 'From dead philology to a living philology'.

But the question of a satisfying life's task still remained open. When Beckh then learned of the preparations for the founding of the Movement for Religious Renewal, he decided there and then to join the founding group. Here the possibility was opened through the words and language of a renewed rite to find a completely new access to the word and to the sounds of speech. And he recognized that something of a future Christianity was wanting to come into being, was what he desired and intuited since as a 16-year-old he had attended a performance of Wagner's *Parsifal* in Bayreuth. Thus he was one of the oldest of the 48 personalities who in September 1922 with Rudolf Steiner's help called The Christian Community into life.

Still during the same year, Beckh moved to the newly built Urachhaus in Stuttgart. In the group of colleagues he took a special position from the beginning. Unlike the others, he was not a priest serving a congregation, but could engage his strengths in free activity as a tutor in the Seminary, as lecturer, researcher and writer and still celebrate the sacraments at various locations. This freedom to study enabled him also to attend lectures at the Goetheanum in Dornach, to contribute in cultural contexts such as the Schopenhauer Society and the Astrology Association, for he was concerned to represent the aspects won out of anthroposophy wherever people wanted to hear them.

The themes on which Beckh lectured ranged widely. Initially, proceeding from his academic work, considerations on language and presentation of Eastern traditional wisdom. Soon he began to concern himself with questions of music, particularly the music of Wagner and the essence of tonality and its connection with the forces of the stars, making his realm of study these stellar forces in the sense of a renewing of early Egyptian wisdom in astronomy and astrology. He sought to discover the cosmic lawfulness of the zodiacal influences in their various effects and reflection in all areas, in the ancient languages and their sounds, in music and the colourful circle of musical keys, in the Mystery wisdom of earlier epochs of human history, in the Gospels and in human destiny. Thus his life's work did finally reveal a uniform thread.

Beckh was not a bookworm, but a human being with an impulsive temperament and a heart capable of enthusiasm. The little chores of daily life often presented obstacles but his being and striving was always directed to the highest; thither he aimed to steer the thoughts of his listeners. With Rudolf Steiner and the Goetheanum he felt deeply connected. Experiencing the Christmas Conference 1923 in Dornach of the General Anthroposophical Society, and his presence at Rudolf Steiner's 'Last Address' to the members on 28 September 1924 (in GA 238) he felt as the climax of his life.

After he died on 1 March 1937, after a difficult period of suffering (cancer of the kidneys), Friedrich Rittelmeyer said of him, 'A singularly unique scholar, a rare wrestler for the spirit, an enthusiastic spirit-prophet has completed his rich life and has inscribed his name forever into the moving history of our time'.

The Works of Prof. Dr Hermann Beckh

'An abundance of books came into existence whose significance perhaps will only be properly appreciated in the future.'
　　　　　　　– Lic. Emil Bock, 'Hermann Beckh' in *Zeitgenossen Weggenossen Wegbereiter*, Stuttgart: Urachhaus 1959. 132

Die Beweislast nach dem Bürgerlichen Gestzbuch (The onus of proof according to the code of civil law)
Prize essay, awarded distinction from the Law Faculty the University of Munich
München and Berlin 1899. Download: http://dlib-pr.mpier.mpg.de/m/kleioc/0010/exec/books/%22103926%22/

Ein Beitrag zur Textkritik an Kalidāsas Meghaduta
(A contribution for the text criticism of Kālidāsa's Meghaduta)
Doctorate dissertation approved by the Department of Philosophy of the University of Berlin 1907.

Die tibetische Übersetzung von Kālidāsas Meghaduta
(The Tibetan translation of Kālidāsa's Meghaduta)
Edited and with a German translation, Berlin 1907/2011.

Beiträge zur tibetischen Grammatik, Lexikogaphie, Stilistik und Metrik
Habilitationsschrift. Berlin 1908.
(Contribution towards a Tibetan grammar, lexicography, style and prosody)
Inaugural dissertation.

Udānavarga
A collection of Buddhist sayings in the Tibetan language. Berlin 1911 (also a recent reprint ed. by Walter de Gruyter, 2013).

Verzeichnis der tibetischen Handschriften
Catalogue of Tibetan MSS in the Royal Library in Berlin (Vol. 24 of the Manuscript Catalogue.) First division: Kanjuar (Bhak-Hgyur).
Berlin 1914/2011/14.

Buddha und seine Lehre
(Buddha and his Teaching). Vol. 1: The Life. Vol. 2: The Teaching.
Sammlung Göschen. Berlin & Leipzig 1916. Third edition 1928.
Later one-volume editions, Stuttgart: Urachhaus 1958/98/2012.
Tr. into Dutch (1961) and Japanese (1962).
Eng. tr. *Buddha's Life and Teaching*, TL 2019.

'*Rudolf Steiner und das Morgenland*'
in *Vom Lebenswerk Rudolf Steiners*
Ed. Friedrich Rittelmeyer. Munich 1921: Chr. Kaiser 1921.
Reprint by HP, Univ. of Michigan (www.lib.umich.edu)
(www.archive.org) Eng. tr. in *Hermann Beckh and the Spirit-Word*, Anastasi 2015. 33-65; also in *The Source of Speech*, 16-71.

—*Der physische und der geistige Ursprung der Sprache*
The Physical and the Spiritual Origin of Speech
Stuttgart 1921.
—'*Es werde Licht!*'
'Let there be light!'
The Biblical Primal Words of Creation. Stuttgart 1921.
—*Etymologie und Lautbedeutung*
Etymology and the Significance of Speech Sounds
in the light of Spiritual Science
Stuttgart 1922/2013.

All three essays on language (above) reprinted in
Neue Wege zur Ursprache, Stuttgart 1954.
Eng. tr. *The Source of Speech*, with all relevant essays articles and articles.
Temple Lodge 2019.

Anthroposophie und Universitätswissenschaft
'Anthroposophy and University Knowledge'
Breslau 1922. Eng. tr. in *Hermann Beckh and the Spirit-Word*, Anastasi
2015. 71-101; also in *The Source of Speech*, TL 2019, 181-207.

Vom geistigen Wesen der Tonarten
*The Essence of Tonality: An attempt to view musical problems in the light of
spiritual science*. With diagrams. Breslau 1922. Third edition 1932. Eng.
tr. with *The Parasifal=Christ=Experience*, TL 2022.

Der Ursprung im Lichte
Our Origin in the Light: Pictures from *'Genesis'*. Stuttgart 1924. Eng. tr.
'Genesis' in *From the Mysteries*, with 'Zarathustra'. TL 2020, 5-53.

Von Buddha zur Christus
From Buddha to Christ
Stuttgart 1925 (Tr. in Norwegian, Oslo 1926) Eng. tr. of short digest:
Floris Books 1978. New Eng. tr. of full text, with additions, 'Steiner and
Buddha', TL 2019.

Das neue Jerusalem
'The New Jerusalem'
A poetic work, in the collaborative work *Gegenwartsrätsel im Offenba-*
rungslicht ('Problems of the Present in the Light of Revelation'), Stuttgart 1925. Eng. tr. in *Alchymie*, TL 2019, 100-13 and *John's Gospel*, TL
2021, 358-372.

Der Hingang des Vollendeten
(Buddha's Passing)
The narration of Buddhas' farewell to the Earth and Nirvāṇa (Mahapa-
rinibbanasutta of the Pali canon).
Translated into German and with an Introduction. Stuttgart 1925/60.
Eng. tr. in preparation.

Zarathustra
Stuttgart 1927. Eng. tr. in *From the Mysteries*, with 'Genesis'. TL 2020,
57-116.

Aus der Welt der Mysterien
From the Mysteries. Seven articles (reprinted). Basel 1927. Eng. tr. (triple
volume) with 'Genesis' and 'Zarathustra'; TL 2020.

Der kosmische Rhythmus im Markus-Evangelium
Mark's Gospel: The Cosmic Rhythm
Basel 1928/60/97. Eng. tr. TL 2021.

Der kosmische Rhythmus, das Sternengeheimnis und Erdengeheimnis im
Johannes-Evangelium
John's Gospel: The Cosmic Rhythm—Stars and Stones
Basel 1930. Eng. tr. TL 2021.

Das Christus-Erlebnis
The Parsifal=Christ=Experience in Wagner's Music Drama
Stuttgart 1930. Eng. tr. with *The Essence of Tonality*, 'Richard Wagner and Christianity' (1933) and essays by Emil Bock (1928) and Rudolf Frieling (1956). TL. 2022.

Vom Geheimnis der Stoffeswelt (Alchymie)
Alchemy: the Mystery of the Material World
Basel 1931/37/42/2007/13. Eng. tr. with Appendices: 'Snow-White' and 'The New Jerusalem', TL 2019.

Der Hymnus an die Erde
From the Old Indian Atharvaveda.
A memorial to the oldest poem and to the early Aryans.
Translated into German and commentary. Stuttgart 1934/60. Eng. tr. in preparation.

Psalm 23 aus der Heilige Schrift
(Psalm 23 from the Holy Bible)
Newly translated into German from the original text and set to music (op. 7).
Stuttgart 1935.

Die Rosen von Damaskus
(The Roses of Damascus)
('Thibaut von Champagne'). The ballad by Conrad Ferdinand Meyer. For solo high voice with piano accompaniment set to music (op. 8). Stuttgart 1937.

Die Sprache der Tonart
The Language of Tonality in the Music from Bach to Bruckner, with special reference to Wagner's music dramas. Stuttgart 1937/87/99.
Eng. tr. Anastasi 2015; TL forthcoming 2022.

Richard Wagner und das Christentum
'Wagner and Christianity'
Stuttgart 1937. Eng. tr. incl. in *The* Parsifal *Christ-Experience in Wagner's Music Drama*, with essays by Emil Bock and Rudolf Frieling, TL 2022.

Indische Weisheit und Christentum
(Indian Wisdom and Christianity)
Articles: 10 reprinted and 9 from the literary estate.
Stuttgart 1938. Eng. tr. in *Collected Articles,* TL 2022.

The Mystery of Musical Creativity: Man and Music
A recently discovered history of music in MS 'Der Mensch und die Musik'.
Five chapters pub. in three articles by *Der Europäer,* Basel 2005/06/07-08.
http://www.perseus.ch/archive/category/europaer/europaer-archiv
Fully restored text translated into Engish, TL 2019.

The Language of the Stars: Zodiac and Planets in Relation to the Human Being
with a chapter on the *Anthroposophical Soul-Calendar (1911-12)* (1930-33)
by Prof. Dr Hermann Beckh
and
The Cosmic Rhythm in the Creed: for readers of Beckh's books (1930-31)
by Dr Rudolf Frieling
with an Introduction and Reviews by Rudolf Frieling and others
Translated from the German by Maren & Alan Stott
Edited by Neil Franklin. Temple Lodge Publishing 2020.

Collected Articles of Rev. Prof. Hermann Beckh (1922-1937).
Over 70 items translated into English, tr. M. & A. Stott, ed. Neil Franklin, TL forthcoming (2023).

Biography:
Gundhild Kačer-Bock. *Hermann Beckh: Leben und Werk*
Hermann Beckh: Life and Work
Stuttgart 1997; Eng. tr. TL 2021.

Two further publications:
Hermann Beckh and the Spirit-Word: Orientalist, Christian Priest, Independent Scholar. Anastasi 2015. Introductory Volume to the *Collected Works,* containing: 'Rudolf Steiner and the East', 'Anthroposophy and University Knowledge', 'Meeting Rudolf Steiner', and profuse appreciations by Beckh's colleagues.

Festschrift: Essays in Honour of Hermann Beckh (2016)
on the Centenary of *Buddha und seine Lehre*
and the publication of the English translation *Buddha's Life and Teaching*
also the first publication of Beckh's *The Mystery of Human Creativity: The Human Being and Music*
and the English translation of Gundhild Kačer-Bock's biography *Hermann Beckh: Life and Work*. Anastasi 2016, TL forthcoming.

Contents includes:
Prof. Hermann Beckh: 'Steiner und Buddha' (1931; previously unpublished)
Prof. Hermann Beckh: 'Buddhism and its Significance for Humanity' (1928)
Prof. Hermann Beckh, 'The Little Squirrel, the Moonlight Princess and the Little Rose', illustrated by Tatjana Schellhase
Johannes Lenz (Berlin): 'Prof. Hermann Beckh'
Manfred Krüger (Nuremberg): 'Daniel Simeon and Asita the Sage'
Oliver Heinl: 'Prof. Dr Hermann Beckh—Pioneer linguistic work in the light of Christ'
Susana Ulrich-Alvarez Ulloa (Öschelbronn): 'The Search for the Lost Word'
Katrin Binder (Nottingham): '*Buddha's Life and Work* one hundred years on'
Alan Stott (Stourbridge): 'Hermann Beckh: Musician' (a lecture, Dornach, April 2016)
Rosemaria Bock (Stuttgart): 'Recollections' (with photos)
Gundhild Kačer-Bock (1924–2008) Memories & Appreciations
Neil Franklin (S. Devon): 'Up the Stairs: Hermann Beckh & the Divine Feminine 1921-29'.

Useful Sources:
Archiv Christengemeinschaft <archiv@christengemeinschaft.org>;
www.rudolf-steiner-bibliothek.de (holds an almost complete collection of Beckh's writings);
bibliothek@goetheanum.ch

Endnotes

1 This essay never appeared separately. The content appeared as separate sections to every key in *Die Sprache der Tonarten* (1937), Eng. tr. *The Language of Tonality*, TL forthcoming 2022—*Tr. note.*

2 Fig. 1 is taken from *Die Sprache der Tonart* (Urachhaus, Stuttgart 1999), in which Prof. Beckh develops observations on the 'crosses of keys', mentions more musical examples and includes references to Wagner's works for each key.

3 For an account of Beckh's life and work, see Gundhild Kačer-Bock, *Hermann Beckh: Life and World,* TL 2021; also Neil Franklin, 'Farther Up! Hermann Beckh: Passing through four levels of consciousness, 1916-1931', in Hermann Beckh, *The Language of the Stars,* TL 2020, pp. 503-20.

4 This is by no means the same for all. So there would be nothing more incorrect, for example, than to attempt superficially to test the following considerations by choosing quite arbitrarily any piece of music. The question is obviously if, and how far at all, the chosen composer felt tonality as understood here. We often find it lacking in second and third-rate composers; they choose their keys more or less indiscriminately. An inner feeling for tonality must always baulk at this, as at the many normally arbitrary transpositions of pieces—especially Lieder. There are absolute rights and wrongs; the key of a composition is not a matter of indifference for its spiritual content and spiritual effect.

5 Here too we can distinguish between composers who to a certain extent command all the keys, who move in them all with the same certainty—they may have a special affinity and preference for the one or the other, like Bach for D-major, Beethoven for F-minor, C-minor and the like—and those who for certain individual keys feel at least this deep and secure instinct. Supreme masters like Bach, Beethoven, and Wagner show this complete security in their choice of keys. These three have achieved a comprehensive command of *all* the keys to a marked degree. In this connection Bach's *Well-Tempered Klavier* (*WTC*), for example, is important and valuable. Other composers move more in a restricted circle of keys which expresses more their own characteristics. Thus Mozart preferred the 'clear and cool' keys around C-major, whereas Chopin preferred the romantic and mystical keys, like D♭-major, A♭-major, B♭-minor, F-minor—C-major, G-major, and so on, meant less to him and were used much less.

6 Dr Erich Schwebsch, *Anton Bruckner, Ein Beitrag zur Erkenntnis von Entwickelungen in der Musik.* Stuttgart, Verlag Der kommende Tag, 1921, p. 97.

7 'I wander'd in forest gloomy…', *Liederkreis* (Heine), op. 24, 3. The setting of the third verse is in G-major—*Tr. note.*

8 In our materialistic age it appears necessary to answer the objection that 'in the southern hemisphere the course of the seasons is exactly reversed'. We should emphasize that just as the relationships of the northern hemisphere are not the only possibility, so here the circle of keys under study is not the only one. There are other chromatic-enharmonic circles of keys with opposite tendencies of movement (see Fig. 2). It is true that the Earth's sleeping and waking, its rhythm from the spiritual to the physical state, affects different places on the Earth's surface differently at any one time. When in our northern latitudes at Christmas nature sleeps most deeply in winter numbness, the spirit of the Earth is widest awake. Alternatively, at St John's-Tide nature is at its highest point and the spirit of the Earth in deepest sleep. In the southern hemisphere, however, the relationships are the opposite. Towards the poles the above-described relationship is balanced out towards the spiritual, and around the equator, towards the physical. Apart from the geographical and historical preponderance of the northern continents over the southern hemisphere in mankind's development, it is important to grasp aright the whole spiritual distinction of North and South, to understand why in such a study we begin with the northern hemisphere. The southern hemisphere being then spiritually negative, requires in our considerations a corresponding spiritual reversal.

9 The visible astronomical change occurs usually around the 21st of the month, but the inner spiritual change is felt a few days later, round about the 24th. For this reason we celebrate Christmas and St John's-Tide not on the first day of winter or summer, but a few days later: 24th/25th December and 24th June.

10 What is here presented should not be understood so superficially as though a composer wishing to express in music, for example, the spell of May, has to choose the key of G-major, or when concerned with musically expressing the experience of midsummer, then A-major. The warmth and light of May can find its expression very well in the warm E-major (e.g. Schumann's '*Mai, lieber Mai, bald bist du wieder da*', op. 68, no. 13), or the bright A-major, the key of tender, heavenly blue. Although the year has not yet reached its heights in May, the Sun has not climbed to its 'loftiest height', it may be said from a certain sensitivity for nature that this comes musically in May to its 'loftiest height', that is, stands in A-major. The crucial point in laying hold of the whole concept always lies in this spirit and not in some other externals. All we can say of the external connection is, that the spiritual position of G-major in the circle of keys relating to the Sun's yearly course corresponds to the position the Sun takes in May. The spirit of the key of G-major itself may not be allotted just to May in a too-external one-sided way. This observation appears necessary to meet the materialistic criticism that deals solely with externals.

[11] Dr Schwebsch first drew my attention to the spiritual significance of this transition from B-major to D-major in his essay on Goethe and Wagner in *Bayreuther Blättern* (republished by Der kommende Tag, Stuttgart).

[12] E. Schwebsch, op. cit., p. 103.

[13] We do not mean by this that it always has to be so, of course. Both movements of the great Fantasia and Fugue in G-minor for organ end in G-major. [Beckh appears to have used Czerny's edition of Bach's *WTC*, in which the Fugue in G-minor ends in the minor, unlike modern critical editions in which it ends with a Picardie-third—*Tr. addition.*]

[14] A random choice of hymns from *The English Hymnal*: O little town of Bethlehem (Forest Green), Once in Royal David's City (Irby), Now thank we all our God (Nun danket); The summer days are come again (Soll's sein); Come, ye thankful people come (St George)—*Tr. note.*

[15] The slow movement of Beethoven's *Pastoral Symphony* is written in B♭-major, the subdominant of F-major—*Tr. note.*

[16] See H. Beckh, 'Es werde Light—Schöpfungsurworte der Bibel' (1921); reprinted in Hermann Beckh, *Neue Wege zur Ursprache* (Stuttgart 1954), pp. 75-109. Eng. tr. 'Let there be Light' in *The Source of Speech*, TL 2020, pp. 154-80.

[17] Absent from the third German edition, 1932.

[18] Prepared by the translator, 2021.

[19] This essay was written for the 50th anniversary of Wagner's death, 1933; first pub. in English in *The Christian Community Journal*, 1933. Tr. rev. A. S.

[20] See: Friedrich Rittelmeyer. *Reincarnation—Philosophy, Religion, Ethics.* Edinburgh. Floris Books 1988; Emil Bock. *Wiederholte Erdenleben. Die Wiederverkörperungsidee in der deutschen Geistesgeschichte.* Stuttgart. Urachhaus. 1967⁵.

[21] See: Hermann Beckh. *The Essence of Tonality.* TL 2022; Hermann Beckh. *The Language of Tonality.* TL forthcoming 2022.

[22] Further details in: Hermann Beckh. *John's Gospel: The Cosmic Rhythm, Stars and Stones.* TL 2021.

[23] Emil Bock. 'Götterdämerung und Auferstehung' in *Die Christengemeinschaft*, Vol. 4, 12. März 1928. 367-72. Eng. tr., 'Twilight of the Gods and Resurrection', see Appendix III.

[24] '*Bühnen-Weihfestspiel*': 'sacred stage festival play', or 'stage dedication festival play', coined by Wagner for this music drama that brings sacred experience on to the stage. Mike Anderson (*Parsifal.* ENO Opera Guide 34. London & New York 1986) suggests 'festival work to consecrate a stage', namely Bayreuth. *Parsifal* sums up Wagner's life's work. In their essays surveying that life's work, H. Beckh and E. Bock (see Introduction and Appendix III) both point to the emerging Mystery-themes in Wagner's work in the light of a non-sectarian Christianity. This theme is presented in detail in Hermann Beckh's *The Language of Tonality*, TL forthcoming 2022—*Tr. note.*

[25] 'Consciousness-soul' is a technical term of anthroposophy for the human member in which recognition of 'what is' as far as what is eternally true begins to light up through reflection (R. Steiner. *Theosophy*; R. Steiner. *Esoteric Science*). In individual biography, the opportunity for its development normally arrives between the years 35-42. The historic birth in the late fifteenth century (anticipated by some outstanding individuals) is confirmed by changed attitudes at the root of many developments in civilization and culture, sometimes summed up as a down-to-earth 'onlooker consciousness', cf. the voyages of discovery, the birth of nation states in Europe, the appearance of perspective in the visual arts, the Renaissance and Shakespeare (above all the figure of Hamlet, in the world's most discussed play, thought by some to be a self-portrayal of the author), the advent of experimental science, and, not least, the birth of the major-minor system in music—*Tr. note*.

[26] In the last lecture given in Torquay, 22 Aug. 1924 (*True and False Paths …* GA 243), Rudolf Steiner spoke about Wagner's *Parsifal*. He emphasized that the music does not yet achieve that musical expression of the Christ-Impulse which would increasingly be the case in Mystery art of the future. Steiner explains how the *Incarnation of Christ* can one day be expressed in notes and intervals. What he says in detail about the 'area of the third', the 'area of the fifth', the 'area of the seventh' and the 'vanishing of the discords of the seventh', and about the 'intimation of a minor experience in the major experience' and about the 'permeation of the area of the fifth and the minor third area' can be related note for note, interval for interval, fairly exactly to the *Last Supper Theme* in Wagner's *Parsifal*. This connection would also exist even when we would have to admit that in his exposition Steiner was *not* thinking on Wagner's theme, perhaps did not even have it consciously in his memory, and that he developed the construction of such a theme purely from spiritual research. The connection meant here as something purely spiritually objective becomes all the more significant in this particular case. [An accurate tr. of the passage from Steiner appears in Lea van der Pals, *The Human Being as Music*. Tr. A.S. Stourbridge 1992. 71-3. Rev. ed. Anastasi. 2014. 120-23—*Tr. addition*.]

[27] For further details, see Hermann Beckh, *The Essence of Tonality*. Tr. A. S. TL 2022; also Hermann Beckh, *The Language of Tonality*. Tr. A. S. TL forthcoming.

[28] We can find in these six notes what, as the musical expression of the theme of the Incarnation of Christ, Steiner called the 'permeation of the area of the fifth with the area of the minor third' (see Note 8 above). Through the adjustment of D♭ to D♮, the key of A♭-major appears pushed into a sphere of C-minor, which becomes still clearer when the same theme is later harmonized in Act I, in the Grail celebration.

[29] This has to do with what Steiner meant by 'the permeation of the area of the fifth in major with the area of the third in minor', as we have already seen within the A♭-major theme itself.

[30] For further details, see Hermann Beckh, *The Essence of Tonality* and Hermann Beckh, *The Language of Tonality*, TL forthcoming. It is shown how F#-major/ G♭-major forms the transition in the circle of keys between the seven keys above and five keys below (between the light keys with sharps and the dark keys with flats), and how in the relative keys, especially E♭-minor, the gravity of the 'spiritual threshold experience' is expressed. Bach's Prelude in E♭-minor in *The Well-Tempered Clavier*, Book I, and Schumann's music to Byron's *Manfred*, op. 115, shows this sense of admonishing seriousness reminiscent of the 'spiritual threshold' of the key of E♭-minor. In *Twilight of the Gods*, in *Tristan and Isolde* (Act III), and in *Parsifal*, Wagner repeatedly allows us to experience in this key the seriousness of crossing the threshold—or, as with Amfortas, also the 'faltering at the threshold'.

[31] Elsewhere, Wagner shows that where it matters he, too, has counterpoint well under control when his musical style demands it. At another point he brings the 'Faith Motif' itself, in the episode with the swan in Act I, into a delicate contrapuntally woven development.

[32] Emil Bock quotes a remarkable saying of Justinus Kerner. *'The eyes are wholly under the heart's sway,* and any suffering which befalls the heart, especially repressed grief, influences them completely. Animals who have the fastest and strongest heartbeat have the most beautiful eyes too, e.g. the falcon, the eagle. The heart *breaks* (*bricht*) and the eye *glazes* (*bricht*), felt and seen simultaneously' (quoted in Emil Bock, *Vorboten des Geistes*. Verlag der Christengemeinschaft. Stuttgart 1929. 147). This observation points very much in the direction we have to seek for the secret of Wagner's chromatic motif in *Parsifal*.

[33] Cf. Albert Steffen on this, *Der Künstler und die Erfüllung der Mysterien.* Dornach 1928/64. 169ff. ('The Artist and the Fulfilment of the Mysteries').

[34] The sentence of Nietzsche runs as follows: 'Richard Wagner, apparently the most victorious, in reality becomes a rotten decadent, driven to despair, suddenly sunk to his knees before the Christian cross, helpless and broken' (*Nietzsche contra Wagner*; Eng. tr. *The Case of Wagner, Nietzsche contra Wagner* … Dodo Press 2008; Createspace 2013, etc.).

[35] With the 'two knives' we are immediately reminded of the 'cutting silver' which plays a role among the Grail symbols (cf. W.J. Stein, *The Ninth Century and the Holy Grail*. TL 2009. Germ. orig. *Weltgeschichte im Licht des Heiligen Gral*, Vol. 1. 189, 219). In the sketch for the cover of [the German edition] of this book by Margareta Woloschin (Stuttgart) this motif appears combined with Wagner's 'Gaze Motif'. A third theme closely connected to it is to be found in Luke 22:38, where the secret of the 'two swords' is touched upon, the illuminating flashes of the spirit-eye (in the Gnostic sense). Cf. 'the mighty vision of two swords of light flashes forth in the lightning rent heaven … two glittering sheaves of light rays' (Emil Bock. *Studies in the Gospels*. Vol. 2, No. 20, p. 176. Edinburgh. Floris Books 2011).

[36] Note here how the theme beginning in the key of the loftiest heights, the Grail heights of radiant A-major, reaches the chord of E♭-major, the lowest point on the circle keys, the circle of fifths, with the word *Tor* ('simpleton'), returning then to the heights through D-minor and G-major, to close on a chord of D-major. This is the key of 'achieving the loftiest heights' which we also meet at the end of Act III when Parsifal mounts to the kingship of the Grail, reaching thus the climax of his life. We see the Parsifal theme, transformed according to the whole development of Parsifal through different keys from its first appearance in the youthful B♭-major episode of the swan in Act I, appearing finally in brilliant, victorious D-major. In this short theme of the prophecy 'made wise through compassion', magically effective in its brevity, the whole 'star-circle' of keys finds musical expression in minature, a 'star-Mystery', to which Rudolf Steiner refers: *Christ and the Spiritual World: The Search for the Holy Grail*, Lectures 5 and 6, Leipzig, 1 & 2 Jan. 1913 (GA 149).

http://wn.rsarchive.org/Lectures/19140101p01.html

[37] Here, with 'Did not the woodland beasts approach tamely and greet you innocently as friends?' is also, incidentally, the place where the 'Faith motif', appearing in the Prelude so primitively, is delicately woven about contrapuntally. Together with the following, 'What did the birds sing to you from the branches?' it is one of those intimate places from which Nietzsche, actually during the period of his opposition to Wagner, said that Wagner had understood as nobody else had, how to contain within the smallest span, an 'eternity of sense and sweetness'.

[38] In a similar way, the plant thus reveals its etheric nature, that is that which is not materially-spatial, in the way it passes through processes in time with its progressive stages of growth and becoming. Here, in this observation of plant growth, we lay hold of the etheric nature not yet *visually*, yet in a process of thought. If we transform thinking into spiritual vision—only made possible today through some kind of 'walk to the Grail Castle', as through recourse to those methods Rudolf Steiner describes in his book *Knowledge of the Higher Worlds: How is it Achieved?* [GA 10] also pub. as *How to Know Higher Worlds*—then temporal experience stands before the spiritual eye as seemingly spatial. Such a spiritually spatial view lies behind all discourse on an 'etheric body': 'You see, my son, time here becomes space.'

[39] Steiner describes this 'walk to the Grail Castle' in the experience of falling asleep at night, as an *approaching the mysteries of the etheric body*. 'Because we are dealing with events which all occur in time, you feel like a traveller making for his own ether-body' (R. Steiner. *The Effect of Occult Development upon the Self and Sheaths of Man*. GA 145).

http://wn.rsarchive.org/Lectures/GA145/English/RSPC1945/OccDev_index.html).

He explains further how in this etheric image-world of the night, images of all the Grail symbols (sword, the lance dripping blood, and so on) appear, as does the *image of the Grail Castle*, in this etheric image experience. To the question, 'What is the Grail itself?' Steiner gives a meaningful answer in this context, leading into the depths of physiology.

[40] In some piano reductions, which aim to 'make the music really easy' for the 'beginner at the piano', these discords are simply glossed over.

[41] Wagner added something else to the letter to Mathilde Wesendonck: 'And I should accomplish something like that? And even write music as well—thanks very much! Let him who wants to, do it. *I* don't want to touch it with a barge pole!' What he then (1859) thought unattainable, was accomplished twenty years later (1877-1882) and with the music.

[42] In his remarkable essay, Emil Bock shows how the Johannine theme of the *transition from father to son* (as the transition from the [Saturnian] revelation of death to that of life, from necessity to freedom, from the law to grace), cf. John 3:35: 'The Father loves the Son, and has given all things into his hand'—is manifested in different ways in Wagner's music dramas. There the forces of the inheriting son are shown in many ways as weak, and they at first break down. In *Parsifal* all this lies between Titurel as the representative of the father-forces, and Amfortas, the failing 'son' (see Appendix III).

[43] This is called the 'astral' [= 'starry'] region in many spiritual traditions, not only in anthroposophy. The contexts which this term introduces cannot be followed up here. Details about it can be found in the author's book, 'Genesis' in *From the Mysteries*, TL 2020, 18-20.

[44] As an initial hypothesis, contradicting Wagner's words, we shall think here not of the dark Herodias herself, the irreconcilable opponent of John the Baptist (as Isabel was the opponent of Elijah), the representative of incurable evil, but rather of the daughter of Herodias, who once prompted by her mother, begged for the head of John the Baptist on a silver charger. This personality is called *Salome* in the legend. Complete conscious evil does not live in her as it does in Herodias. She is only a 'hierodule', a temple courtesan in the field of influence of these dark mysteries, where she serves the purposes of the adversary through the spell of her demonic female charm. Through giving herself to this she loses her ego, her self, to the adversary. There she becomes the spineless instrument of alien black-magic spells [cf. all this in the author's, *Mark's Gospel: The Cosmic Rhythm*, TL 2021, 131ff.].

[45] Rudolf Steiner once pointed out that in the Grail world, too, a pair of adversaries is involved: Klingsor and Iblis.

[46] It was pointed out above that we should not think of Herodias herself but of the daughter of Herodias.

[47] She goes about it in a similar way as another one, a personality lying, it appears, within the sphere of Herodias, the Syrophoenician [Syrian